trust within

Molly Carroll

ALSO BY MOLLY CARROLL

Cracking Open

trust within

Letting Intuition Lead

From the author
of *Cracking Open*

MOLLY CARROLL

Published by Grand Harbor Press, Grand Haven, MI

www.brilliancepublishing.com

Amazon, the Amazon logo, and Grand Harbor Press are trademarks of Amazon.com,
Inc., or its affiliates.

ISBN-13: 9781503942073
ISBN-10: 1503942074

Cover design by Faceout Studio

Printed in the United States of America

This book is dedicated to my husband, Adam, for his unending love, support, and exceptional editing skills.

And to my children, Tommy and Cora, whose natural ability to tap into their intuition is a gift.

I love you.

Contents

PROLOGUE

Travelers, there is no path, paths are made by walking.

—*Antonio Machado*

We all struggle. You may be struggling in your marriage, or with being honest about the way you treat your body. You may be confronting an addiction or beginning a divorce. Wherever you are facing a challenge, I want you to know you are not alone. These challenges have also touched my life, but where I have struggled the most is in my relationship to my mind—my ruminating, comparing, and incessant mind. Buddhists named it the monkey mind, therapists diagnose it as anxiety, and I call it hell.

Ever since I was young I have spent several of my waking hours worrying about being included or excluded, a thought pattern that revolves around being seen, yet feels so lonely. When I was a kid, my angst was around questions like "Will I be invited to the slumber party?" and "Will someone like me?" and "Will I be one of the chosen few for dodgeball?" As I have grown, these worries have changed, but only a bit: "Will he or she be mad at me?" "Did I do or say something wrong?" "Why did that person give me a weird look in yoga class?" My mind has always been my battlefield, and I am on the front lines.

I think I hide it well. I don't think my therapist or close friends and family really know how much I have struggled with the cycling thoughts every day. My Times Square ticker tape of words, words, words constantly running through my brain, robbing me of peace—crucifying me in my place of ease.

I hide it well because I am high functioning and work hard at everything. My whole life I have been teased for getting more done before 6:00 a.m. than most of my friends would do in a whole day. But secretly what I am doing is running away from my mind, running away from the stories that plagued my waking hours and trying to escape being in bed with, quite honestly, myself.

Yet I know that my mission to have a loving relationship with my mind brings healing. I cannot tell you how many times when a yoga teacher asks my class to set an intention mine has been peace of mind. Or how often when I am in church I beg and pray to God to release me from the grip of anxiety. Or how on my morning runs I try to imagine all my fears and worries are pouring out of my feet and into the ground to be dissolved in Mother Earth's womb.

I meditate, I go to therapy, and I attend spiritual circles to look deeper into this addiction, disease, diagnosis, dysfunction—whatever you want to label it—just to function in the world, and it all helps. It really helps.

But one thing has helped me more than anything else; it is free, and with me all the time. It is my saving grace, my god, my golden ticket, my medication, and my Holy Grail. It is my intuition. The word "intuition" comes from the Latin word "*intueri*," which is translated as "to look inside" or "to contemplate." *Merriam-Webster* explains it as "a natural ability or power that makes it possible to know something without any proof or evidence." It is known as a "gut feeling," an unconscious experience that encourages one to do something without logically knowing why. Even though you may not know why you are hearing this voice or having this experiential feeling, it is important to listen to it and also ask yourself, "How will this voice or feeling affect my life and all those around me?" Let your morals, values, and ethics seep into this experience to help guide you towards your next steps. It is a voice that radiates throughout the whole body, and the quieter and stiller you become, the louder it will share its wisdom. The voice may scare you, challenge you, force you to look your fears in the eye, but it will always free you.

Your intuition is a place to land when you are pulling out your hair because you are frustrated with life or lost for answers. When you can find a way to be still, breathe, be present, and simply listen to your intuition, you are freer, and peacefulness follows. Your ticker-tape thoughts may then disappear, your anxiety can soften, and your mind melts a bit.

Sometimes you may hear a loving, calm, assuring voice say, "Go to bed and deal with it in the morning." Or "Get up, go for a walk, make your kids breakfast, give them a hug, and surround yourself with your loving friends or family." Or you may hear a stronger voice say, "Sit your ass down and be with all these uncomfortable, scary feelings. Let them know they don't control you. Make them your friends, not your enemies. Don't hide and don't numb yourself with a drink, a phone call, or a new piece of clothing. No, sit and breathe, and be with all that is arising." Or you may hear, "Get your ass up, dance, sing, be in nature, but do not wallow anymore. This will not serve anyone, especially yourself." And ultimately you may hear from your sweet inner voice, "You are not alone—we all struggle. It is what gives you the gift of empathy and the ability to connect to other human beings, nature, and God." Suffering is part of your journey; you have to embrace the dark shadow of your suffering to get to the root of your intuition. In these moments you will feel so separate, but remember you are never alone—you are always connected to your higher power and your heart. My intuition has stayed true to me, and I have learned to trust it entirely.

Even though intuition is an imperative part of my life, how did I come to write a book on this expansive and elusive topic? One crisp fall afternoon I was in a meeting with a reputable publishing house at a high-rise in midtown Manhattan. The women were asking me about my previous book, *Cracking Open*, and my work as a therapist and public speaker. "What did you talk about in regards to trust?" one of them asked, referring to a concept I'd discussed at a conference.

"Intuition," I said, "because I have always trusted my intuition."

The women looked at each other and smiled. "Would you ever write a book for us on intuition?" another asked.

This was one of those life moments where time stops and you know your stars are aligned. As a struggling writer, I was frozen with shock at this opportunity, but I simultaneously had a deep conviction that my career as an educator, writer, and therapist, and my personal healing work for years, had prepared me for this opportunity. And so I said yes. Or I should say I was a bit tongue-tied, so my agent said, "Molly would love to write a book on intuition."

So I went on a quest to learn more about intuition, and in doing so I found new truths. I discovered that I can give myself away in order to avoid feeling lonely, scared, or left out. I would pick up the phone to call someone, or spend time with people and in places that did not fill my soul. Or I would mistreat my body by eating frozen pizzas and chocolate into the wee hours to fill my space of loneliness. After giving myself away or sabotaging my body, I would end this abuse with a "shame attack," saying, "Molly, how could you do this, say that, or make that decision." This may sound pathetic, but it was my truth, and to start living more in intuition you must be honest.

I discovered not only where I could give myself away, but also what I need to do to live in my truth. I need to surrender to the dark, uncomfortable emotions of my fears to awaken to more light. I learned that when I am honest and still, I hear the wise voices of those guides, ancestors, angels, and most importantly myself, who will lead me to my inner truth. I learned that when I allow myself to embrace the expansion and contraction of life, the ebb and flow of my days, I am a less anxious person, a stronger mother, a more loving partner, and a more available therapist. On this pilgrimage I have pledged not to sell my soul in order to feed my addiction to being liked. I will not send emails, make phone calls, or be unauthentic to get my high of "I'm okay, because you say I am okay." I am not going to let my mind control my heart. And I learned that to live wholeheartedly, I must allow my intuition to be my compass of truth.

I wish for you to come along with me on this journey, and I wish for you to be a truth teller, to walk the walk, and to listen to your heart. Struggle, grow, love, or laugh as you may—I give you permission to stop allowing your wounds to define you. To stop giving away your body, money, or soul to please another. To only follow your one truth, your intuition.

INTRODUCTION

Great Mystery, teach me how to trust my heart, my mind, my intuition, my inner knowing, the senses of my body, the blessings of my spirit. Teach me to trust these things so that I may enter my sacred space and love beyond my fear, and thus walk in balance with the passing of each glorious sun.

—*Lakota Tribe*

We must all face our truths on the path of change, and in order to transform, we have to recognize that being honest is part of the journey. A journey with many twists and turns. A journey that will encompass the births and deaths of our loved ones, and of ourselves. A journey where we're sometimes the student, sometimes the teacher. A journey where one day we are laughing and dancing and the next we may be crying. A journey packed with lessons to learn in our homes, classrooms, and offices, and on the streets—lessons that don't always come easy.

Intuition is the tool that makes the path of change navigable, and it's one of the most powerful decision-making tools you wield, so why not tap into it every day? What if you made your choices around your own gut feelings or hunches? What if you lived every day using your analytical mind *with* your intuitive heart? What if you did not succumb to the fear around your "shoulds" and "coulds"? Today is the day to answer these questions. Today is the day to be honest about the life you have been living, the life you can live, and the life you *want* to live.

Let me guide you on your journey to discover your intuition, that mysterious and subtle gift that the mystics and sages have studied for centuries, and that psychologists and theorists continue to study. As a mother, writer, therapist, educator, and public speaker, my greatest strength is drawing out the best in people. On stages, in conference rooms, and in my private practice, I always encourage my clients, students, and audiences to trust their inner voices, play with the uncertainties of life, and listen to their deeper wisdom that is uniquely their own. More importantly, as a student of intuition myself, I have become more honest about my struggles and challenges, and I've gone against the voices of those who have questioned my decisions. For instance, I left my children and husband for three weeks to volunteer with Tibetan refugees in India, where I received a personal audience with His Holiness the Dalai Lama. And I married an atheist even though I was raised Catholic.

Trust Within is for anyone who wants to become more honest about *their* choices and challenges, and to lift the veil of daily life to glimpse deeper truths. It is for people who don't want to live in the status quo anymore, people who are open to spontaneity and surprise. It is for people who can recognize how the choices made by listening to their hearts and heads will help their communities, colleagues, family, and friends all rise to become healthier and whole. Intuition is about helping us all awaken to be our best selves together. It is for anyone asking themselves these questions: "Should I buy this plane ticket to travel to India?" "Should I stay in my job?" "Why did I cheat on my partner?" "Why did I choose responsibility over fun?" "How am I going to make it through one more day?"

You may be asking these questions yourself. Or you may have picked up this book because you want to find out what is best for your soul, or open your heart and mind to new ideas and possibilities and connections, or find further motivation for personal change. Or perhaps you feel lost and need a compass to find your way back home. Whatever you're here for, *Trust Within* will teach you the tools and techniques you need to access your intuition and make better life decisions.

I will also present different philosophical, cultural, and historical viewpoints regarding intuition, which will show you approaches to life from many different perspectives, and I'll share heartfelt stories of people who learned from their intuition and thrived afterward. These brave souls—such as an architect, an addict, a Silicon Valley executive, a psychic, a playwright, and a storyteller—have shown me how many different definitions of intuition there are: intuition is about listening to all your voices, for instance, or paying attention to your bodily wisdom, trusting your heart, or surrendering to life. Their stories will help you open doors of intuition inside you, even when you're tempted to keep them shut out of fear. And yes, there will be fear at first. Following your intuition is not always a concrete path, laid out perfectly before you. But you must soldier into unchartered territory to keep from falling back into old patterns that no longer serve you.

As challenging as following your intuition may be at first, however, you'll be surprised to find how comparatively simple accessing it is once you know how. Amazingly, this powerful tool is at your fingertips. It does not matter what color your skin is, how much money you have in the bank, where you live in the world, or what size pants you wear, the intuitive instinct courses through your veins—it's part of who you are, and it's what connects you to others and to yourself. It's a sort of sixth sense, the closest thing you have to psychic ability, and through it you can discover things you cannot possibly find through your other senses, things you may want to run from because they're so novel, so mysterious.

You must not run, however. Trust your intuition, not only because when you follow it you'll discover how rich and fulfilling the destination may be, but also because it is imperative to do so in today's society.

Everyone wants things instantly. Our children are huddled indoors building virtual worlds on their technological devices, not building forts outside. Instead of writing a piece of poetry or reading a book, we reach for our cell phones, and instead of connecting with others over a cup of coffee, we check how many "likes" we have on Facebook or Instagram. In turn, our real connections—to others and to our own individual souls—suffer. It all feels unnatural, and at a pace unlikely to last.

It was not always this way, of course. Earlier cultures made intuition a priority. They were wise enough to slow down, listen intently, and access their intuition to enlighten their decisions. Despite modern culture's frenetic pace, and despite our fear of detaching ourselves from our devices, there remains a deep longing to recapture this wisdom from our ancestors.

In my office I often witness this desire to slow down. My clients' souls lament the current human condition, and their hearts hunger for deeper meaning. To satisfy this hunger, we must—as individuals, as a society—choose to elevate the importance of our gut instincts. We must ask ourselves, with urgency, "When am I going to start listening?"

Where to begin? With stillness, meditation, space to reconnect with our inner selves, and a decision to find greater fulfillment within ourselves, because the more we long for possessions and external validation, the further we drift from the things that nourish and satisfy our souls. There is so much more to life than material accumulation. Notice that instant high you feel right after you buy something new, anything from a sweater to a car. The high passes quickly, though, and what usually follows is a longing for yet another possession. Material accumulation feeds our ego, our persona, our longing to be seen. Internal inquiry feeds the soul. When you find your place of stillness, you see everything is God, oneness, and interdependent. We are one world, one ecosystem, and one life force that yearns to awaken and be of service to all, not just the individual.

Now is a time of spiritual awakening, a transformation, and a way to look at your life through a different lens. This lens may seem blurry at times, but if you stay on the path and keep your heart in the journey, you will reach a more fulfilling and purposeful life.

All you need and will learn is already deep inside of you. You just need to tap into it, trust it, and learn to live with it. I believe so deeply that intuition is essential for a healthy and happy life, I am on this journey with you. In my life, my family, and my practice I commit myself daily to the pursuit of discovering intuition not only for myself, but also for all the people I work with who strive for meaning and fulfillment.

John O'Donohue—Irish poet, author, priest, and philosopher—said beautifully:

> We live between the act of awakening and the act of surrender. Each morning we awaken to the light and the invitation to a new day in the world of time; each night we surrender to the dark to be taken to play in the world of dreams where time is no more. At birth we were awakened and emerged to become visible in the world. At death we will surrender again to the dark to become invisible. Awakening and surrender: They frame each day and each life; between them is the journey where anything can happen, the beauty and the frailty.

I want to share this gift of surrendering and awakening with you. I want intuition to become a tool to help you make healthy decisions, a place for you to land when you are lost or confused, and an inner sanctuary to go inside to learn more about who you are and what you want in this short and precious life. Take this book in your hands and read the stories so you may know you are not alone in your pain. We all have trials and tribulations—that is what makes us human—but when you do stumble, your intuition will give you a place to fall.

CHAPTER 1

How strange that the nature of life is change, yet the nature of human beings is to resist change. And how ironic that the difficult times we fear might ruin us are the very ones that can break us open and help us blossom into who we were meant to be.

—Elizabeth Lesser,
Broken Open

I will never forget the day my therapist handed me a crumpled piece of paper on which she had written an excerpt from Mary Oliver's poem "The Journey." I was twenty-eight and struggling with ending a relationship with the man to whom I was engaged. He was a wonderful person who appeared on the outside to be a catch. He was successful, handsome, creative, and kind. But inside my heart, I intuitively knew I should not marry this man and that he was not my life partner. My therapist knew it also, and that is why she handed me Oliver's wise words, which helped me finally listen to my intuition to live my one true life.

Are you ready to live the life that is waiting for you? I believe you are. Perhaps for years you have been hearing voices that don't always follow the status quo or what someone else thinks you should do. You know, deep down, that you want to learn how to follow these voices. You want to understand what these nudges mean and how to use them to have a richer life and a deeper relationship with yourself. It is not always easy to follow this calling. You may be afraid, overwhelmed, or convinced you do not have the tenacity to accept this challenge. But keep listening, and you will hear the voices of your soul. Stay strong, have courage, and live in your heart. Come with me. I am waiting for you. Do not put on your running shoes or hide from this life-changing opportunity.

I know this is not always easy. The complications of our daily lives can make it difficult to find time to focus on our intuition and ourselves. There are so many responsibilities: being successful in your career, keeping your family happy and healthy, paying the mortgage, and maintaining stable relationships. Given these obligations, you may be asking yourself, "Why should I spend my time strengthening my intuition?" First, when you trust your intuition you are more productive with your time and energy. Second, when you listen to your heart you are a much more effective decision maker. Lastly, when you tap into your gut instinct you improve your own internal life and you connect to the oneness of all, living in alignment for something much bigger, much more fulfilling.

Life is precious, and I don't know about you, but the older I get, the faster life seems to pass by. I wake up and it is Monday morning and the next thing I know it's Friday. Knowing that our time is precious, why would we want to spend it worrying about our decisions or choices? If you had a magic wand that helped you save time by doing only the things that bring you joy and contentment, wouldn't you use it? Lucky for you, you do have this magic wand; it is called your intuition.

When you make a decision using your intuition, you will not waste time worrying or feeling scared. According to a study in *Psychology Today*, car buyers who pored over all of the information about their various car choices were later found to be satisfied with their purchase only 25 percent of the time. Meanwhile, those buyers who made a quick, intuitive decision about their car purchase were found to be more satisfied with their purchase 60 percent of the time.

Decision making is difficult. It encompasses so many components, including your physical, mental, and emotional well-being, and it is especially challenging when the choices are not clear, or when you know that you may annoy a friend, disappoint a colleague, or upset someone you love. What compounds it all even further is how *many* decisions we must make. Humans often make up to thirty-five thousand decisions in one day, according to *Leading Edge Journal* at Roberts Wesleyan College. Anything from whether you should buy a black sweater or a white one, to whether you should leave a job or marriage that is unfulfilling, to whether you feel you're physically able to run a marathon or emotionally capable of spending time with someone. Who wouldn't want some support and guidance in this process?

I understand. Even though I love to live in my intuition, I can still bang my head against the wall over decisions: Should my kid be in one extracurricular program or another one? Should I confront a friend who hurt my feelings? What can I do to help my mom on her days of chemotherapy? But then I remind myself that my brain is battling my heart, and I must let go of control and let intuition guide me. Questioning myself incessantly, writing out the pros and cons, asking friends and family for advice, making calculations on a spreadsheet—the things humans do to prove to ourselves that our decisions are sound—won't help me. Deepak Chopra, alternative-medicine advocate, speaks of this:

> If you obsess over whether you are making the right decision, you are basically assuming that the universe will reward

you for one thing and punish you for another. The universe has no fixed agenda. Once you make any decision, it works around that decision. There is no right or wrong, only a series of possibilities that shift with each thought, feeling, and action that you experience.

Practice and Pay Attention

The more you listen to your heart and trust that the universe has your best interests in mind, the more confident you will be in your decisions. Intuition is like a muscle: the more you use it, the stronger and more reliable it becomes. Once you start to live this way, you begin to trust your choices are made from a place of security, not insecurity. When you are secure in your decisions, you have fewer regrets and less guilt, and in turn you are able to direct more precious energy toward your passions. Think back to a time that you made a snap decision that you were proud of. That was coming from your intuition. Now think of a time you made a decision after reviewing all the facts and figures, taking time to analyze every detail. How did that turn out?

For his commencement address in 2016 at Harvard University, filmmaker Steven Spielberg gave a speech encouraging graduates to follow their intuition:

> Your education and experience is designed to build you to a place where you can start making decisions for yourself and trust your intuition. If you want to be the hero of your own story, rather than a supporting character in someone else's, you have to get to a point where you can listen to that intuition.

When Spielberg was a young adult, he knew what he wanted to do, but he did not know who he was. And how could he? Like many of us, for years he had listened to the voices of his parents and professors, and then his employers and mentors. He was not all that different from other young adults. Spielberg explained how at first this voice—the voice of his intuition—was barely audible, but as he started to pay more attention to it, the voice grew louder and his intuition became stronger. He went on to say:

> And I want to be clear that your intuition is different from your conscience. They work in tandem, but here's the distinction: your conscience shouts, "Here's what you *should* do," while your intuition whispers, "Here's what you *could* do." . . . Once I turned to my intuition, and I tuned into it, certain projects began to pull me into them, and others, I turned away from.

This address is a perfect representation of how listening to your intuition will help you hear what you *could* do instead of what you *should* do.

From Intuition to Service

Making decisions from your intuition is beneficial for you, and it is beneficial for the world. Following your intuition has a domino effect: Once you begin to care more about your own livelihood, you care more about the environment, other cultures, political strife, and global travesties. Once you stop tolerating the injustices in your own life, you stop tolerating the injustices in other people's lives as well. Once you find you cannot just throw away a plastic water bottle, or take a plastic bag from the grocery store, you may stop supporting items made in a country without child-labor laws.

When you develop a strong practice of living in your intuitive heart, you have more compassion for others and have a harder time participating in gossip or entertaining judgmental thoughts. I first learned how to listen to my intuition to serve others from the prayer of Saint Francis. As a young girl attending Catholic school, I would go to Mass two or three times a week. As I was wiggling in the wood pews, I would simultaneously hope and pray we would sing my favorite hymn from the prayer of Saint Francis, "Make Me a Channel of Your Peace." With this hymn I could tap into my heart and spread my love to my classmates, family, and anyone I ran into during and after Mass. I am not sure exactly why, but each time I sang it with my raspy voice, my entire body filled with joy, and I intuitively knew that Saint Francis's words were turning me into an advocate for others. Each time I left Mass, I wanted to be a better person, a kinder soul to all those around me.

> *Lord, make me an instrument of your peace. Where there is hatred, let me sow love; where there is injury, pardon; where there is doubt, faith; where there is despair, hope; where there is darkness, light; where there is sadness, joy.*
>
> *O, Divine Master, grant that I may not so much seek to be consoled as to console; to be understood as to understand; to be loved as to love. For it is in giving that we receive; it is in pardoning that we are pardoned; it is in dying that we are born again to eternal life.*

When you listen to your heart, as I first did in that pew all those years ago, you tap into your instinct to love others. Your life and work then become infused with this instinct, allowing you to grow and to spread grace everywhere you go.

Inspiration from Successful Examples

Now that you know that living in your intuition will save you time, help you make better decisions, and have a unifying effect on the world, isn't it clear why thought leaders, CEOs, and athletes take this research to heart? By listening to their internal voices, they have found some of their most profound successes.

Richard Branson and Oprah Winfrey are just two CEOs who pride themselves on making some of their best decisions from their gut instincts. Intuition is her muse, Oprah said. "Follow your instincts. That's where true wisdom manifests itself." Richard Branson said, "I rely far more on gut instinct than researching huge amounts of statistics."

Steve Jobs spoke about how following his intuition led to Apple's success and about how he often witnessed intuition at work in other countries. "The people in the Indian countryside don't use their intellect like we do," he said. "They use their intuition instead, and the intuition is far more developed than in the rest of the world. . . . Intuition is a very powerful thing, more powerful than intellect, in my opinion. That's had a big impact on my work. Western rational thought is not an innate human characteristic; it is learned, and it is the great achievement of Western civilization. In the villages of India, they never learned it. They learned something else, which is in some ways just as valuable but in other ways is not. That's the power of intuition and experiential wisdom."

We see intuition's power not only in the business world, but in sports as well. Imagine driving a car at two hundred miles per hour—the speed of Formula One drivers. One driver shared a story with the University of Leeds about going that fast and braking sharply at a hairpin curve without knowing why. As a result he avoided hitting a car pileup right around the corner, which undoubtedly saved his life. The driver said his urge to brake was simply stronger than his desire to win the race. Later, as the driver watched a recording of the event, he noticed that the crowd that would have normally been cheering for him was not even looking his way—their focus was frozen elsewhere. He was not conscious of the crowd's distraction while he was on the track; he just knew then that something was not right.

When you love something wholeheartedly, you help the object of your love grow. Intuition is the same: if you develop a love affair with its wisdom, spend time with its gifts, and make it an integral part of your life, it will grow, and you will not betray yourself anymore. Others' betrayal is painful, but betraying yourself is much worse. You can hear if you are betraying yourself. It will sound like "I feel as if I am giving up my inner power. I am compromising my beliefs and values. This is costing me my psyche and soul." Yet when you live in love and intuition, you will not betray yourself, and instead you will hear, "I feel strong in my decisions, I feel safe with my partner, and I feel secure in my life." Then you will know you are devoted to yourself and your inner voice.

Trust Your Intuition

I hope these stories and studies give you the comfort of knowing that there is proof in the unprovable. You want control over your life. Control makes you feel safe. But the funny thing is that you don't really have control—at least not over the outcomes. No matter how the numbers add up—no matter how many times you go over your options, say your prayers, review your pluses and minuses—you cannot control your outcomes. But we do have choices, and you can trust that life has a way of teaching you what you need to learn when you need to learn it. If you can trust you are following something bigger—something outside the box, something neither concrete nor analytical—you will discover bliss.

Being inside your intuition means time stops and you get clear answers to your questions, clear solutions for your quandaries, and deep comfort for your emotional pain. You've been inside your intuition before. Just think about a time you had a hunch that you followed and it turned out great for you. Or remember for a moment the death of a loved one or a failure in your career or as a parent; afterward you may have heard a voice that spoke some comfort or advice to you. Or you felt something in your body—a pull in your gut, sweaty palms, or a racing heart. And you may have said a quick prayer or encountered an energy that gave you support, guidance, and answers that helped you get through. In each of these moments you tapped into your intuition. When tapped into more regularly, this power will help you make some of the best decisions of your life.

"You were born with wings," the Sufi poet Rumi said. "Why prefer to crawl through life?" I know you have wings and are ready to fly. Trust that your intuition is the wind that will lift you out of your slumber and help you soar. Believe that voice in your heart is the power that will help you get to where you need to go.

So why follow your intuition at all?

- Follow your intuition for the practicalities of life: saving time, making solid decisions, and being of service to the world.
- Follow your intuition as an educator and help others make stronger decisions by teaching them the practical intuitive tools you have used to better your own life.
- Follow your intuition as a parent, teacher, aunt, or uncle, and help children strengthen their emotional-intelligence skills, the same way you'd help them bolster their math and reading skills.
- Follow your intuition as a human being who struggles with feeling left out, insecure, scared, ugly, fat, or lonely. When you find yourself trapped in the dark cave where those feelings dwell, use your intuition to guide you toward the light of self-compassion. Life is sometimes hard, yes, but your intuition will serve as a constant reminder that you are truly loved and that you are free to accept your flawed yet beautiful self.
- Follow your intuition to cultivate gut-instinct habits. Your intuition will support your decision to leave a party when you don't feel safe anymore, to not attend a college that

doesn't feel right in your soul, to hire someone that may not be perfect on paper but is a perfect fit for your company, or to take a job that fills your heart and not just your wallet.

- Follow your intuition to learn that life is not about pleasing others, or being accepted by everyone, but rather about radiating your joy for life out to all those around you.

How do you reach this sacred place, develop these valuable skills? You will find throughout these pages many tips and techniques, but the best way is simply to become quiet and open to all that you feel, hear, and experience. Have a hungry heart. Yearn for creativity and inspiration and to drink the nectar of life. Do not stay comfortable in your negative patterns and behaviors. Make intuition part of your web of life, the quilt you go to bed with at night, and the recipe you cook with to nourish your soul. Your life is too precious to sit on the sidelines and not follow your intuitive heart. It is your time. Your passions and callings deserve to be pursued.

CHAPTER 2

*The sun shines not on us but in us. The rivers flow not past, but through us,
thrilling, tingling, vibrating every fiber and cell of the substance of our bodies, making
them glide and sing.*

—John Muir

Your intuition can speak to you in many ways. It may inspire you to
create a piece of art, or a new company. It might encourage you to leave
a toxic relationship or a city that is stealing your soul. Or it may put a
fire in your belly to fight for a cause, to stand up against something that
may be controversial. This type of intuitive voice is called the intuition
of advocacy. I believe you have a place deep inside you that wants to
fight for something bigger than yourself, a place magnetically pulling
you toward something that speaks to your heart. Your fight may be one
others support and admire you for, or it may make people uncomfortable and cause them to question their values and choices. Your passion
won't let others' opinions influence or stop you from moving forward,
however. By answering your calling, you will change the trajectory of
your life.

The intuition of advocacy is the voice you hear deep inside that summons you to do something for the greater good, to change the world. That voice may tell you to fight cancer because it touched you or someone you loved. Or it may tell you to stand against racism, sexism, or economic inequality for young girls and women because you or someone you love suffered abuse, judgment, or trauma. The intuition-of-advocacy voice could tell you to do anything from picking up a shovel to plant a community garden on a concrete slab to fighting for child-labor laws in an overseas factory. The voice is part of your soul's code. It tells you what you came into this world to do, to fight, to accomplish.

As you become an intuitive advocate, you will face your fears. You must—otherwise you will not grow. You will confront parts of yourself that you've ignored because you've become so accustomed to your everyday behaviors. You will bump up against your persona, the parts of yourself that you most closely identify with—the leader or servant, the child or parent, the married or divorced—and you may notice you are scared to change that role. You may also collide with your psyche and the parts of yourself that are too uncomfortable to explore more deeply. But I give you the gift of breaking free from your prisons, confronting what scares you most, and becoming closer to your "God." Your "God" is the essence of your soul, which is the whole reason you fight for a cause in the first place.

Listening to your intuition of advocacy can be a lifelong practice. You may transform into something else with age, wisdom, and experience. Take John Francis, a man who followed his heart, challenged his fears, and listened deeply to his intuition of advocacy to fight for the environment and its sacred soul.

Intuitive Guide: John Francis

One day I heard someone on the radio interview John about his journey with the environment, silence, and walking the planet. The moment

I heard his story, I thought to myself, "Who better to talk to about intuition than a man who was silent for seventeen years and walked the planet for twenty-two?"

As I prepared for our interview, I found myself squirming on my bar stool at my kitchen counter. I wanted to make sure I was ready when I received that odd ring from Skype. I fumbled with my keyboard, straightened my shirt, and checked that my lipstick was not smeared. I was a bit anxious and intimidated because I would be talking with a man who has a deep and rich well of knowledge around listening to his intuition.

The moment John and I connected on Skype, all my nerves disappeared. I instantly noticed his warmth, even over the computer. His inviting smile and quiet demeanor created an environment of connection. I could talk to him as if I had known him for years. He shared stories about his wife, and I saw his son pop in and out of the screen, which created an assurance that I was talking to the right man, at exactly the right time.

I began our conversation with a question about what intuition means to him. He sat back in his chair with a contemplative look. "Words are interesting," he said. "'Intuition' is like trying to say something that is unsayable, like trying to explain silence. I fly all over the world trying to talk about silence. 'Intuition' is another word like 'God' that means something, but we are unable to say it."

Intuition is murky and hard to define because we are attempting to assign words to a feeling. Trying to figure it out can make your hairs split with frustration.

John Francis was born in Philadelphia, the son of a West Indian immigrant. As a young adult he found his way to Marin County. On January 19, 1971, he witnessed two oil tankers collide beneath the Golden Gate Bridge. From this atrocity, more than half a million gallons of oil spilled into the bay, leaving thousands of birds and sea life-forms coated in toxic black smudge. In this devastating moment, John's sixth sense flooded into full gear. He shared in his book, *Planetwalker*, what happened to his body after the oil spill: "The sickly sweet smell of oil hidden in the morning fog drifts up from the water. My head swims and my stomach churns the way it did when I was a kid squeezed between two fat Philadelphia relatives in the backseat of a hot summer car—air conditioner failing, windows barely open." John did not only feel this oil spill in his body, but also in his heart. He said he felt some responsibility for the mess washing up onto the shore.

You may be able to relate to John's story. Has there been a moment in your life when you felt the same intense body sensations? This is usually the first sign of your intuition of advocacy. You may witness, hear, or read about an event, and then your body begins to respond in a way that is out of the norm. Your response may be quite dramatic: you may shake uncontrollably, cry from the depths of your belly, have a deep pull to scream or crawl out of your skin. Or the internal experience may be very subtle: you feel uneasy, almost nauseous, or as if something is just not right. Your body is telling you that what you just witnessed is something on your path of life that you need to make a priority if you want to create some sort of change.

Once John saw the devastation from the collision, he woke up to the sacredness of the earth and the close relationship between our hearts and the environment. He was so disturbed by what he witnessed that he decided to give up riding and driving in motorized vehicles. This was a bold decision because he lived in Inverness, California, a small community of (at the time) 350 people on the Point Reyes Peninsula. To get anywhere he needed to drive.

"More or less I couldn't think of what to do," he said. "I had a friend die in a boating accident, and after the death I decided to walk twenty miles, and on that walk I thought, 'This is the only thing I think I can do to raise environmental consciousness and promote earth stewardship.' I didn't know where it would lead me, but I knew I needed to do it." John's intuition came in such an unconscious way, but what is admirable is that when he heard these callings to walk, he listened, and walked.

People would drive up to him and ask, "John, what are you doing?" and he would say, "Well, I'm walking for the environment." And they would say, "No you are walking to make us look bad, right? You're walking to make us feel bad." He admits that maybe there was some truth to that, but he believed that if he started walking, everyone would follow, because they would feel the same pain he did about the oil, or pollution. But people didn't follow his campaign, making him even more infuriated, turning his peaceful mission into a toxic mess. He found himself arguing with people over his cause.

This reaction is not uncommon. When your intuition of advocacy begins and you strongly believe in something, it's not unusual to come from a place of anger, or to want to prove something to others. You may find you have a deep fight in you, which can powerfully propel your cause forward. But I caution you to avoid letting this "fighting" voice come off to others as adversarial, because it may paint you as someone "shoving" your cause in others' faces, which may turn people away from you rather than invite them on your journey.

As they did with John, people may question your cause and examine your values and choices. Generally this is because when someone shines a light on an issue, everybody—be they roadside picketers or disagreeable friends and family members—have to look at it on a deeper level, which is not always comfortable. People don't like to see the shadow side, the dark parts of life. Having to wake up and really look at someone's cause can be excruciating, because many of us are drawn only to the light, to the parts of life that make us feel okay about our everyday decisions. Look at what is going on with our planet, for example. It can be eye-opening to have to question how many plastic bottles you are using, airline flights you are taking, or resources you are abusing. When a challenging view confronts you, your brain's prefrontal cortex may become flooded with emotions, which can lead you to a state of fight or flight. You will then fight for or against a cause or walk away.

Once you go through the difficult process of awakening to the truth of your own or someone else's intuitive advocacy, a monumental sense of freedom follows. And, beautifully, people begin to support the pilgrimage for change. We cannot fight alone.

John eventually realized he needed to stop fighting. On his twenty-seventh birthday, he decided he had argued and talked enough, so he was going to stop speaking for one day. He got up one morning and did not say a word. "I believe the silent path that I embarked on was brought about by following my intuition," John said. "It was a very moving experience because for the first time, I began really listening. And what I heard disturbed me."

He paused, maybe reflecting upon the lessons he learned during his days of silence. "What I used to do was I would listen just enough to hear what people had to say, and it was in that moment that I stopped listening. In my mind, I raced ahead and thought about what I was going to say back while they were finishing up, and then I would launch in. . . . What I was doing was ending communication. I thought I knew everything, and I didn't."

Indeed, intuition is not only about listening to your own sixth sense, or gut feeling; it is about listening to others. From their words your intuition is formed on a deeper level. Many people don't really listen, because they are too preoccupied with what they are going to say next, with getting their own opinions across. And that only puts a blockade between people. When you are already thinking about what to say next, your intuition is unable to come through and energy can't flow freely.

I am not immune to this problem. I listen to my children's stories or about their quandaries, and I am already thinking of what to say next to fix their problems. I probably want to fix the pain I feel for them just as badly as I want to help. At times I sit in my therapy chair and instead of listening without an agenda, a theory will pop into my mind, which keeps me from truly listening. We can only help others develop their own intuition when we sit with them in their sadness and successes, open our hearts, and listen without agendas or solutions for the other person's problems. Only then can they comfortably share their full thoughts and emotions, and through this process their intuition has space to breathe and expand.

John's wake-up call inspired him to take listening to a whole new level. He was silent for another day, and another, until after being silent for a year he realized he was learning more and more every day. Keeping silent was a vow he reassessed one year at a time. Each year on his birthday he would ask himself, "John, are you going to keep this up? Are you going to keep walking and not talking? Should I talk today or this year?" This monastic lifestyle lasted for seventeen years. Each year that his inner voice told him to be silent, he trusted that voice and knew that by doing so there was more for him to learn about himself and his environment.

Reassessing your intuitive advocacy is about staying curious about your cause. Ask yourself, "What is the earth calling me to do and say, where is my energy most useful, and how am I following my spiritual path?" Give yourself up to what needs to be done. By staying receptive to what life is trying to tell you, you are welcoming your clairvoyant knowledge instead of filtering only what your fears want to hear. Being an advocate doesn't always look like you thought it would, or may want it to look like, but this intuitive excursion is not about comfort; it is about cracking yourself open to the unknown and, with compassion and insight, diving deep into your well of wisdom.

When John cracked himself open and stayed that way, his gut told him to stay quiet and keep walking. But one day he heard, "Go back to school." He began his educational journey—oh no, not by plane, car, or train, but by walking five hundred miles to Ashland, Oregon. After receiving his bachelor's degree from Southern Oregon University, he wished to receive his master's degree from the University of Montana. After receiving his acceptance letter, he wrote to the University of Montana to let them know he would be walking to Missoula, which meant it would take him a bit longer to arrive at his first day of class. It took him two years.

John received his master's, then proceeded to do something I had never heard of before: he taught a class without speaking. "I had thirteen students when I first walked into class," he said. "A friend of mine who could interpret my sign language told the class that I was John Francis and was walking around the world. I didn't talk, and this was the last time she was going to be there to interpret for me."

My jaw dropped open, and we both laughed a little. "I could see they were looking for their schedules to see when they could get out of my class," he continued. "Two weeks later, everyone was trying to get in my class. What I learned from teaching in silence was that sometimes I would make a sign and my students would say things that I absolutely did not mean, but I should have meant. The silence was the best teacher."

Once you choose to follow your intuition, you will usually hear your deepest wisdom during silence. That wisdom can come in through the body, or from another person, but silence is a very powerful force in the realm of intuition; similar to how when you water a plant it will grow, spending time in silence will help your intuition grow as well. By being silent you will often hear what you need to do or say. When fighting for a cause, we often think we must be on a stage, with a megaphone, shouting for what we want others to hear, but as you can see in John's story, silence was his best voice to fight for his cause. And after seventeen years of it, two years writing about oil spills, years of scholarship to receive his PhD in environmental studies, and seven years to walk across the United States, John began to feel it was time to share what he had learned. "The later years have become more comforting, and silence more familiar," he writes in his book, *Planetwalker*.

"Meaning is rooted in action and lives." On his forty-fourth birthday, after seventeen years of silence, he received his calling that it was time to talk. In 1990, on the twentieth anniversary of Earth Day, John began to speak. "I have chosen Earth Day to begin speaking," he wrote, "to remind myself that now I will be speaking for the environment."

John spoke of the environment in his TED talk by reading a quote by Lynton Caldwell in the textbook *Living in the Environment* that captured why John was on his pilgrimage. "The environmental crisis is an outward manifestation of a crisis of mind and spirit. There could be no greater misconception of its meaning than to believe it to be concerned only with endangered wildlife, human-made ugliness, and pollution. These are part of it, but more importantly, the crisis is concerned with the kind of creatures we are and what we must become if we are to survive."

John started talking because he had studied the environment at a formal level. But he knew there was an informal level as well. At the informal level, he learned about people. He wanted to speak about what he learned from the environment; he had more to talk about than trees, endangered species, or global warming. After walking across the United States and meeting all walks of life, he wanted to talk about people and how we make up the environment. "We are the environment," John said in his TED talk. "It is about how we trust people and about having a mutual understanding about what we are all talking about in the environment. Such as sustainable living, gender equality, and human rights. The most important part of the environment is the way we relate to one another."

In Jungian psychology we call this the collective unconscious, an ancient part of the mind that calls you to action, summons you to be a voice for the silent, and makes you feel connected to humanity. On September 11, 2001, for example, we as a human race all felt the devastation of what occurred in New York City, not just the ones who lost loved ones or lived there. This awful act of terrorism deeply affected the collective unconscious of everybody.

After everything John had experienced, little did he know that one of his greatest teachings was still ahead of him. During John's sacred pilgrimage, he walked through El Dorado, a prison town in Venezuela. A prison guard pointed an M16 at him and said, "*Passaporte, passaporte.*"

"Passport, huh?" John responded. "I don't need to show you my passport. It's in the back of my pack. I'm Dr. Francis. I have my PhD. I'm a UN ambassador, and I'm walking around the world." As he started walking off, he asked himself, "What possessed me to say such a thing?"

And then, as if he were channeling a fellow intuitive advocate from beyond, he heard the words "Free at last, free at last, thank God Almighty, I'm free at last." John had had a realization: even though he was on a path to free others, he was not totally free himself. He was still imprisoned in his own mind, in his man-that-walks-the-planet persona. He had never stopped to ask himself, "Is this who I want to be?" And by wondering it for the first time, he realized he had a responsibility to more than just himself.

John knew then he needed to change, but he was still afraid. He was so used to identifying as the guy who walked, he did not know who he would be if he just stopped. But deep down he knew he needed to leave behind the security of his old self to become a new self. His intuition let him know he needed to free himself from his prison, as comfortable as it may be, and do something new.

"I think whether I speak or not, intuition for me remains the same," John told me. "It is about following our life's path. The more experience and learning we have, the more opportunities we have for making change."

I believe John meant being an advocate to help change the world, the environment, and ourselves. Whether we like it or not, change is the natural rhythm of life. When we accept that, and when we follow our intuition and act with more self-love and less shame, we take the risks we need to.

How often are we "John," where we don't stop ourselves to ask the big life questions? "Who am I?" "What do I want from my life?" "Why am I doing the things I do?" If we don't question, we stay in a jail of an unexamined life.

What do you know needs to change in your own life but you struggle with it anyway? Before you overwhelm yourself with it, stop, get quiet, and connect to something in the environment—a tree, the ocean, an animal. Feel its essence, and notice the sensations in your body. Now ask yourself, "What is the greatest good for me, and the planet, in this moment?" What answer do you hear?

Every day in my clinician's room I see clients convinced they know exactly how their journeys will play out. The thought of changing course rocks them to their core. But I nevertheless have the gift of witnessing the beauty of their transformation. After twenty years working with families and children, I believe most people change so they can connect more deeply with their friends and family, and ultimately with themselves. Deeper human connections, and opportunities for change in general, occur when we open our eyes and hearts to our deepest vulnerabilities. Talk about being an advocate! How amazing would it be if we were all advocates for deeper connection?

John taught me intuition has a depth that we cannot always see from the surface. When you first become an intuitive advocate, you may see just the tip of the iceberg. John's iceberg tip was to walk and be silent. And then he began to go deeper and it changed: he began to hear "Now walk and go to school," then "Walk and speak for the environment." And now he's reevaluating because he realizes his cause is about more than just an oil spill; it is about having a responsibility to the environment of human connection, and to ourselves.

As my conversation with John ended, I breathed a sigh of gratitude. His wisdom, silence, sore feet, open heart, and activist spirit left me with a sense of freedom, as I am sure they do with many others. He reminds us that if we want to be advocates for the environment, a disease, or a cause, we must tap into our intuition at each twist and turn and always remember that in order to make a difference we must exercise the core practices of intuition: be open to change, follow a passion at all costs, humble oneself to see beyond the ego for the greater good, and shut up and start to listen.

CHAPTER 3

CONNECTING TO YOUR INTUITION THROUGH SELF-AWARENESS

At the center of your being you have the answer; you know who you are and you know what you want.

—*Lao Tzu*

"To thine own self be true," Polonius says to his son Laertes in *Hamlet*. Polonius is encouraging Laertes to not deceive himself by ignoring what is true in his heart. By becoming more aware of his own heart, he will become more true to all those around him. Polonius is teaching his son about self-awareness.

Self-awareness is key to intuition. When you are more in touch with yourself, you have a clearer pathway to your intuition. You don't question your gut feelings or premonitions, because you trust yourself so deeply that you know your truth.

Self-awareness is one of those words like "intuition"—hard to define. I have discovered as a therapist and seeker that self-awareness is about knowing wholeheartedly who you are, and what you are curious about in life. It revolves around knowing how to function in the world with an inner courage, even in the face of adversity, risk, and fear. Through self-awareness you don't allow things to keep you from determining which decisions need to be made, and you don't spend as much time and energy worrying about who you should be or what you should be doing. Self-awareness is about making confident choices, choices that help you become more emotionally transparent, vulnerable, and authentic. And from this place of awareness and worth, you have a backstage pass to your intuition.

Reaching this place of self-awareness is easier said than done. The way our culture is set up, we don't always know what is best for us. As Americans our sense of worth often revolves around how big our house is, what type of car we drive, what schools our children attend, and where we vacation—superficial reflections of self that rob one's spiritual access to greater self-awareness.

This robbery is not limited to our possessions. Technology plays a role, too. While today we can stay more universally connected to others around the world and see our friends and family in an instant, our computers, smartphones, and other devices are also dictating our level of happiness and worth. We are slowly training ourselves to value our self-worth by how many "likes" we have when we post a picture or story. I have seen clients in tears when someone defriended them online.

With all this chatter and noise, how do you find the silence you need in order to grow more fully into your sense of self, to walk in the world with more truth, positivity, and love for yourself and others? First commit to walk the pilgrimage of honest self-reflection: notice where you hold yourself back, downplay your gifts and graces, and give away your power to others because you are too scared to honor what you are worth. This journey is about strengthening your belief that you know what is best for you—even when your family, bosses, friends, and society are telling you something different—and teaching you a simple lesson: how to trust yourself.

The lesson begins with small but effective choices. Unplug from your technology, social media, or cell phones for a while each day.

Spend more time healing yourself in nature. Stroll along a stream, hike a mountain, walk in the woods—or even just among the trees in your neighborhood. Surround yourself with people who support your being, your true essence, and with whom you know you can be your whole self. Continue to challenge the fears that hold you back from deepening your sense of self. Allow space for stillness through yoga and meditation, which will help you tap into your intuition, this one still voice that will always remind you that you are a gift and should be valued as such.

On my quest to discover people who exemplify a strong sense of self and therefore have a deep connection to their intuition, I came across two intuitive guides who have quite contrasting lifestyles yet share such a similar internal philosophy about how self-acceptance can enhance one's intuition. I met my first guide as I was walking into a public bathroom one early morning.

Intuitive Guide: Sunny Delight

I was mistaken to assume that the custodian I saw cleaning the toilets was struggling. I bumped into her as I was shimmying between the bathroom door and the "Caution: Floor Is Wet" sign. She looked up at me and said, "Oh, I am sorry," flashing a kind smile.

I instantly knew I needed to talk to her about her sixth sense. "Can I talk to you about intuition?"

"Intuition?"

"Yes," I said. "You know that feeling you get in your gut when you know something is right, and you don't know why it is right, but you feel it in every part of your body?"

"Oh yes, intuition," she said with an accent. "I will talk with you about intuition."

I grabbed my laptop and sank to the bathroom floor to type while she continued to clean.

Sunny Delight, a perfect name for her personality, was born in a remote mountain village in South Korea. She was raised in a home with no electricity or running water, but lots of love. When she was six years old, she and her mother were watching the evening sunset. "Tomorrow is Western New Year on the other side of the world," her mother had said. "Next year you go to school, get educated, so you can see the world." Sunny knew nothing about the world outside of her village, let alone America. "The world is so much bigger than our small village," her mother continued. "You need to go see it."

These words sweetened this young child's soul, and in that moment she was self-aware enough to listen to her intuition, which created a kind of secret world within her, a world where living in the United States someday was a real possibility. She spent hours dreaming in this world. Even though Sunny's family was poor and her odds of living in the United States were low, she was self-aware enough to know that nothing would keep her from believing in her secret.

"I knew I would live in America and see the world," Sunny told me.

Her words reminded me of the connection between dreams, self-awareness, and intuition. During a dream, or even while awake, you may hear your intuition tell you to do this, build that, go there, or create this, or you may not "hear" it at all—you may feel it in every bone in your body. What allows you to fulfill this dream is the self-awareness that you are worthy of having this dream come to fruition.

When Sunny's intuition told her she was to live in the United States, something inside her knew she was worthy of living out her dream. "I did not tell anyone of my plan until I was twenty-five years old," she told me, "and then I tried several times to receive a visa. I had a plan, a dream, and no matter what happened, I was going to see the United States."

Yet time and time again her paperwork was denied, and she did not receive her visa. Then one night she was watching the television and saw a picture of Tom Brokaw, and she heard her inner voice say, "Tomorrow you will receive your visa. He will make it happen." The next day her dream came true.

While telling me this part of the story, Sunny stopped mopping and looked down at me, and we both started to laugh hysterically. We laughed from our souls. Even though we had never met before, and lived different lives, we both knew that it was her soul and her sense of self, not Tom Brokaw, that gave her the strength to listen to her intuition. There, on the bathroom floor, with Sunny standing above me, I had a vision that she was my preacher, singing her sermon of self-awareness, and I was in her congregation, listening with an open heart that had so much to learn.

"I choose to clean the bathroom," she continued. "Because nobody bothers me, I am really good at my job, and when I am done, I am done."

"Do you ever get depressed missing your country or family?" I asked her.

She stopped mopping and looked up at me as if I had just called her a foul name. "Depressed? Why would I be depressed? No. Why be negative? Life is so short; you could die tomorrow. You should be positive." She took a breath. "I wake up every day happy that I have a brand-new day. I don't want to ruin anyone else's day with being sad. Everybody has pain, suffering, and problems." Scrubbing away, she said, "This is the way I see people. Those people who are negative are always looking up and wondering, 'Why don't I have two million dollars, a big house? I want what they have up there.' While positive people look down and think, 'I am so lucky to be able to pay my bills, have food, and I appreciate all that I have versus what I don't have.'"

Her wisdom made me think of the concept of the comparing mind, which can be one of the greatest soul crushers. When you can listen to your intuition, you are self-aware enough to know that if you constantly compare your life to others' and count what you don't have, you will be depressed, whereas if you can appreciate all your gifts—health, family, and friends—your sweet life will become crystal clear. It comes down to having a deep sense of gratitude, pure gratitude.

Sunny Delight continued preaching her wisdom: "I don't care what people say about me. I come from a different country, I clean toilets, and some may say my job is depressing. But it makes me so happy. Today so many people are dying from stress. I am not stressed. Why should I be? I pay my bills, and I have a job. I am happy."

I didn't even have to ask Sunny Delight any questions. Her intuition was on fire, and she just kept on speaking from the heart. "It doesn't matter what you do. Have a plan and go for it. Get as much as you can out of life. I have lived in the United States for twenty-six years and still have a plan, and hope to see more of the world. If you have one education, get another one. I wish I could have more education, but I haven't been able to."

Mop in hand, she began to giggle and spin around like a whirling dervish. "Every morning I wake up and see another day!" Her words echoed off the bathroom tiles, creating a vibration of light in my heart.

Sunny was pacing, and I could tell she had one final thought. "If the doctor told you that you only have three months to live, what would you do? Those months are valuable. You must live those days. People will die today—everyone could die today—and you have to live for this moment." As Sunny packed up her cleaning supplies, I remembered the pity I felt for her at first. "Oh, I wonder if this woman who cleans toilets has a good life," I had thought. I felt embarrassed to admit to myself that this patronizing attitude was so white, so upper class. Then I quickly reminded myself not to judge a book by its cover. This custodian on the outside was a self-aware Buddha on the inside. Was I ever wrong to think that Sunny was struggling! She taught me that when you know yourself, you will also know the beauty of being in the moment, being positive, and appreciating all that you have because life is short. She was my intuitive preacher on self-awareness for the day.

Intuitive Guide: Peter Mallouk

I met my next guide in a very different way. I wanted to interview people who had found personal and professional success through self-awareness and intuition, and I couldn't help but think of Peter Mallouk, whose family have been dear friends of my sister's for years.

Peter is the president and chief investment officer of Creative Planning. Creative Planning provides comprehensive wealth-management services, including financial planning, charitable planning, retirement planning, and tax planning. *Barron's* named him the number-one independent financial adviser in America three straight years. And he is the author of *The 5 Mistakes Every Investor Makes and How to Avoid Them: Getting Investing Right*.

Peter's inspiration to develop his successful company came from something close to his heart—his father. His dad was a doctor and frustrated by the financial world, which he felt exploited and took advantage of him. He would have a meeting with his attorney, then his tax accountant, and then yet another meeting with his retirement planner, and in each of these situations Peter's father felt as if they were trying to sell him needless insurance or charge him extra fees and premiums.

After Peter graduated college, he was self-aware enough to know he wanted to relieve people like his father from some of the personal stress the financial world was so good at causing. Intuitively he felt he could create a one-stop shop, where clients could receive support for all their financial needs and feel aligned with their advisers. He thought maybe a few hundred people would be interested in this service, not over twenty thousand.

Peter was not only wise enough to listen to his gut and find a way to help solve a problem, but he was also tapped into his sixth sense enough to know that he could use his interpersonal gifts to make it happen. He knew his company's success depended heavily on whom he hired and how he ran his business, so he surrounded himself with an "inner circle" of people he trusted and admired. He continues to pride himself on the employees he hires and mentors.

"Where I am most intuitive is in the hiring process," he told me. "I hire really talented people. I hire people that don't always fit in a mold. In this area, I lean toward my intuition over my mind. And because of this I have found the diamonds in the rough. It may be people where somewhere else they were not fully utilized or could reach their highest potential. But I talk with them for a while and figure out what my gut is saying." Peter is not only using his intuition; he is keenly aware of doing so.

"There have been several times when I am interviewing someone and they are amazing on paper," Peter said. "They have all the education and experience to work at my company, but something in my gut tells me no, they are not right for the job. And the same goes for the other direction. I may meet someone and they don't have the exact requirements to work with me, but there is something pulling at me that tells me I should hire this person. In both instances I followed my gut."

And when he does not listen to his intuition? "My gut will not let me off the hook." He had to learn this the hard way, by hiring the wrong person or trusting someone for the wrong reasons. "This is yes and this no," he said, referring to how clear cut his gut is. "Where people make mistakes is when they are too overly analytical and ignore their feelings without being mindful. And the same occurs when people let their heart take over when they need to be analytical."

Are you beginning to see a pattern in my intuitive guides? They experience something—an oil spill, a sunset, or a father's strife—and from this experience they have an emotional response: anger, sadness, or inspiration. Then they hear from deep inside their souls they need to take action. Then they are self-aware enough to tap into the deepest level of their intuition and follow this call to action—walking for seventeen years, starting a successful company, following a dream to live in another country.

Here is another opportunity to get out your psyche magnifying glass to look closely at your own self-awareness and enhance your sixth sense. Ask yourself these life questions with as much honesty as you can muster up: "Who am I?" "What do I want?" "What is holding me back from achieving it?" "What does it take to get it?" "Where am I personally and professionally strongest?"

"Have you always been this self-aware?" I asked Peter.

He started to laugh. "No, I have not always been this way. There was a time when I was oblivious. . . . Learning to decipher between your mind, heart, or gut makes you better but not perfect. Nothing is perfect. You can increase your chances to make a good decision when you can discover which of these to lean on, but you will still be wrong ten percent of the time. It's important to accept this as part of life."

Indeed, making mistakes is an important part of self-awareness. Without making them it is difficult to build character, discover who you are, and figure out what resonates with your soul.

"What happens is when you get successful you become more busy and can get overconsumed by your responsibilities," Peter continued. "And with success bad things happen, because you ignore other things in your life. I saw a lot of bad things happen to people around me."

He saw it happening to himself as well. For one, he was saying yes to too many things. "When you get successful lots of opportunities come your way." He would be on six charity boards when he would have rather been home, with his family and people he wanted to be with. "'Wait a second,'" Peter said he eventually told himself. "'I cannot have one million friends. I need to make a radical shift to what and who is really important to me.' From this shift I became really aware and mindful. I now have a handful of close friends. Life is not about speed dating."

What Peter is saying is simple, but so important. We all get busy, but the key to finding balance is to stop, set boundaries, be present, and notice who and what you want in your life. You may have a million followers on Facebook but no one to call when you are lonely. You may have a million dollars in your bank account but feel poor in your soul. Peter became aware of the importance of spending time with people he loves and cherishes, and to him this is true self-awareness.

"Awareness is the key to intuition," he said. "It is about being contemplative about your life so you can begin to notice when something doesn't feel right. If you are really aware, then you begin to notice things about people. And from this mindful awareness you can begin to follow your intuition on who you will spend your time with."

"How do you stay so grounded in life?" I asked, wanting to get to the root of mindfulness.

Even though we were on the phone, I could almost feel a smile cross his face, as if this subject were one of his favorites. "It is easy when my clients are fulfilled and happy," he said. "This is very important to me. My clients are happy because we are not selling them products they are not happy with. It is easy to have energy, because my job is so rewarding. I hire different people who are incredibly talented, and then we teach them our way of being. And I try to stay grounded in my personal life as well. I may have to have forty meetings in one day, but I will do that so that I can be at my kid's sporting or school events. I never want to miss anything. Family is very important to me."

"Is there anything else?" I asked.

"Yes, I sit with clients all day who have made a lot of money. And on a lot of occasions they are the first family member who has ever made a million dollars. So because of this they end up paying for a lot of the family. Some clients complain about this: 'I have to pay for this or that, so and so asked for more money again.' And some do not complain at all. One day I was with a client who never complained. . . . I noticed this and said to him, 'You never complain about supporting your family.' The man paused and then said, 'I'm really blessed to be a blessing to my family.'"

Peter said that he has never forgotten this. The deepest self-awareness lesson he learned is how really blessed he is to be a blessing in his friends' and family's lives. He intuitively and consciously knows this is a blessing. He can do great things with this money, have a great impact on people and organizations, and is so fortunate to be a part of several charities. He referenced the Bible, Genesis 12:2: "I will make you a great nation, and I will bless you; I will make your name great, and you will be a blessing."

For a few moments we were silent, and then Peter softly said, "Everything emanates from that."

In that moment I instinctually knew why I chose to talk to him: he said what we all needed to hear.

What a gift to realize that everything emanates from being a blessing to others. We are all given gifts that we are called upon to share with the world. It may not be money; it could be listening skills, a gift for teaching, or singing. Whatever it may be, you are a blessing to your family, friends, and colleagues, and all fellow humans; you are a gift to this world. Once you tap into your blessings, you become more self-aware, you more readily witness when something moves your soul and inspires you to take action, and ultimately you change the world and bless others.

Sunny and Peter enlightened us on how to embrace that we are all blessings. Their deep sense of self, positive attitudes, passion for people, and life choices taught us how to take blessings and spread them like seeds in harvest time, water them with love, and watch them grow with pride. Thank you, Sunny and Peter, for inspiring us to embrace the idea behind "To thine own self be true"—to not deceive ourselves and instead tap into our hearts and the wealth of intuition inside us.

CHAPTER 4

When you talk, you are only repeating what you already know; but when you listen, you may learn something new.

—*Dalai Lama*

One crisp fall evening a few years ago, I was browsing through Netflix when I became instantly intrigued by a documentary I came across entitled *10 Questions for the Dalai Lama*. "What would I ask the Dalai Lama if I ever met him?" I thought. Luck brought me to the film, and curiosity moved my finger to click the play button.

The documentary is about American director Rick Ray's visit to Dharamsala, India, where His Holiness the Dalai Lama resides in the beautiful Himalayan Mountains. Ray was granted a private interview with the Dalai Lama but was given only one hour. The film gives viewers a window into the unrest of the Tibetan culture while letting us also see an intimate interview with His Holiness. What to ask in such a short amount of time? Ray's questions were intriguing and thoughtful: How do you reconcile a commitment to nonviolence when faced with violence? Why do the poor often seem happier than the rich?

Halfway through the documentary my entire body began to shake, literally shake, and I heard as loud as a church bell on a Sunday morning, "You must travel to India and help the Tibetan refugees." I paused the film and thought, "What is going on?" I started to breathe heavier in hopes of stopping my shaking, and I just let my intuition guide me to a travel website to start looking for airline tickets to India.

In that moment I gained one of the most valuable tools in developing and strengthening intuition: simply to be present in the moment and listen.

Laying the Groundwork

Listening to the call of my soul, I worked quickly to make this trip become a reality. The next month was a whirlwind frenzy of logistics. I booked my ticket to New Delhi, got my kids' schedules settled, worked with my clients to be able to leave for three weeks, raised money to travel and donate to a Tibetan refugee charity, and reserved my hotel rooms, car rentals, and bus tickets. Being present had allowed me to hear the calling to go to India, but it also gave me the organization and dedication necessary to travel through that massively diverse and beautifully chaotic country.

Running on adrenaline, I continued preparing for my journey, until one day tragedy hit: my father died. I was devastated. My intuition was like a gray fog on a San Francisco summer day. I could barely see, feel, or hear anything. I was so stricken with grief, I could hardly get my kids dressed and to school, let alone continue to plan my trip to India. I knew I needed to postpone my journey and heal from the loss of my father. I canceled my trip and just tried to get through each day.

As time heals all wounds, and seasons change, so did my grief. It went from feeling like a ton of bricks weighed on my heart, paralyzing me, to a bag of rocks that I could lift off so that I could walk in the world again, to finally a few pebbles that were always with me but didn't inhibit me from functioning.

The winter passed, and summer came with a renewed energy. One afternoon, while hiking through beautiful wildflowers, a friend asked me, "When are you going to India? You raised money, have all the preparations. You should go."

"It is not that easy to just go to India," I answered, a bit defensive. "I have the kids, my work, and responsibilities."

She challenged me: "All I hear is excuses of why you cannot go to India. You are not listening to the voice you heard that told you to go to India."

It stung, but I intuitively knew she was right. I returned from that hike with my intuition ignited, blazing me back to the original travel site to rebook my ticket. I left three weeks later.

Amid the logistical frenzy I somehow remembered an email I sent to the Dalai Lama the year before, requesting a private audience. I was coming to India to work with Tibetan refugees, I had written, and was there any way I could meet with His Holiness?

A kind man on the other end of the world wrote back: "I am sorry, ma'am, but no. His Holiness is very busy. He is in his seventies and receives hundreds of requests for private audiences a week." Knowing this was a shot in the dark, I kindly thanked him and went on with planning my trip.

Now, as I was again ready to leave for India, I thought, "I am going to email that man again and ask for a private audience."

This is one of the beauties of intuition—it can numb you to the fear of rejection, or it did me. You may have a strong gut pull to do something without thinking about the consequences or the rejection you may face. It is your sixth sense at play, which can be much louder than your ego or rational mind.

While in this unconscious state of intuition, I wrote the kind man a second time: "Hello, it is me again, Molly Carroll. I was unable to travel to India last fall because my father passed away, but I am coming now to work with Tibetan refugees and attend His Holiness's teachings. Is there any way I can have a private audience with His Holiness?"

For a few days there was email silence. Anxiously, I would check my email several times a day, but nothing arrived. But the day before I left for India I received a response: "I will see what I can do." Afterward I experienced what I call "a moment with God." I took my hands off the keyboard, inhaled a deep breath, and felt God all throughout my body. I said a heartfelt prayer of gratitude and said thank you to those in my life who had passed and were now my spiritual guides. I said thank you to God for all that he had given me. I said thank you to myself for all my emotional and spiritual work, which had allowed me to hear my intuition, this call of the wild. And from this call I had the courage to answer "Yes!" when asked to show up in life, yes to an adventure that did not necessarily make sense and meant I had to leave my five- and seven-year-old children, my job, and my life to go on a solo pilgrimage to India. It was not logical. It was a calling straight from the heart.

Going to India

I left for India two days later.

Once I had arrived, my intuition was, as my lovely Southern friend says, "open for business."

I had been in India for about a week when one smoggy afternoon I was yearning to check in with the real world, so I walked into one of the open-air Internet cafés to read my email. My heart almost broke free from my chest—there before me was a message from His Holiness's secretary. I took a deep breath to settle my shaky fingers and opened the email. "Molly, when you arrive in Dharamsala please come find me," it read. I froze, then tried to jump up from my chair, but the sweat from my thighs stuck me to the plastic, and I almost fell over. I pulled myself together, walked out into the bustling streets, and went on with my day.

A week later I found myself at His Holiness's office to inquire about my personal audience. With trepidation I approached the counter and told a quiet yet serious man why I was there. He gave me an inquisitive look. "Give me your number," he said. "I will have someone call you."

I left and heard my intuitive voice tell me, "Molly, you have to let go of this dream. It may not happen. You have a week to be in Dharamsala, and you are here to be with the Tibetan refugees, not just to see the Dalai Lama." The message set me free from my expectations and allowed me to be present and remember why I came to India in the first place.

Hours passed without hearing from his office, so I went back to inquire about the personal audience, my determined—some might call stubborn—attitude in tow. As I again approached the desk, the same man walked toward me and slid a piece of paper into my hands. "Wednesday, 11:30 a.m.," it read. I looked at him teary-eyed and said in barely a whisper, "Thank you."

Meeting the Dalai Lama

Wednesday came, and I did my India morning routine. I took a walk, drank some coffee, wrote a bit, and went to the temple to attend His Holiness's teachings. As our lunch break neared, I noticed it was 11:00 a.m. "I have a few minutes to grab lunch," I thought. I was corralled out of the temple with hundreds of others attending the teachings and found a café just outside the temple gates.

Not being in the most conscious state of mind, I walked into the café and grabbed the first thing I could see. It was a piece of cold lasagna. Yes, you read that right. You may be asking yourself, "Who eats lasagna in India, in hundred-degree heat?" Someone who is going to meet the Dalai Lama in thirty minutes and doesn't care what she eats, that's who.

I ate as fast as I could and noticed it was 11:25 a.m. I could not believe I only had five minutes to get to his residence. I ran as fast as my short legs could take me and arrived at the temple right on time. After going through quite a security process, I was guided into the driveway outside his residence. I instantly felt a calm wash over my lasagna-filled body.

Incredibly peaceful monks guided me and fifteen other lucky souls to an area where we awaited our private audiences. As I stood there, I began shaking like I had the first time I watched the documentary almost two years before. I took a deep breath and closed my eyes, and when I opened them I saw a well-dressed man walking toward me.

He reached out his hand. "Hello, Molly. I am Tenzin. I am the man you have been emailing with."

I had no words to express my gratitude. I just held his hand. "How can I thank you?"

"It is my pleasure."

When the Dalai Lama walked out, Tenzin personally took me to him. "Your Holiness, this is Molly Carroll, whose father died."

As I silently stood next to this wise, enlightened being and held his hands, I suddenly remembered months past, when while in Oregon I woke from a deep sleep and thought, "I had the craziest dream. I dreamed I met the Dalai Lama." Now in real time I was holding his hand, in complete peace. I had to breathe to not pass out. We were silent for a few minutes, and I looked at him and saw that he was look-ing to the sky, bobbing his head quietly, saying, "Oh." Then his calm, angelic voice asked one question: "How old was your father when he passed away?"

"Seventy," I said.

I couldn't consciously comprehend much in that moment, but I knew deep in my bones that my father was standing there with the Dalai Lama and me. Though my father was dead, this was one of the most intimate moments I had ever had with him or any other human being.

I thought I would have had a million questions, but the Dalai Lama and I continued to stand there in silence. Questions no longer seemed to matter. Our time was coming to a close. I expressed my gratitude, we took some photos together, and I dizzily began to leave His Holiness's residence. As I walked down the aged stone path, I collapsed in tears, tears of gratitude for this once-in-a-lifetime experience, tears of grief knowing that my father was with me at that moment, and tears of courage for not listening to the voices that said, "Don't go to India alone as a woman. It is too dangerous." Or "Don't leave your family. It is not a good choice."

No.

I had listened to the deepest part of my soul when it told me, "You must go. It is in your destiny." As I came back to consciousness, I raised my tear-filled face only to see five guards looking down at me awestruck, most likely thinking, "We have a nine-one-one situation here. We have a crazy blonde American woman on the grounds." I found a way to pick myself up, smile at the guards, and walk on knowing that I was just given a precious, transformative offering. By following my intuition and not allowing life's "shoulds" to cloud my Indian pilgrimage, I learned some valuable lessons:

- I learned I could walk the crowded, car-honking, cow-wandering streets with open eyes and a childlike heart.
- I learned to indulge in the exotic curries and succulent samosas with an appreciative palate.
- I learned to open my heart to those suffering immense poverty and pain—women and children begging in the streets, lepers isolated by their affliction.
- I learned about India's unending wealth of compassion and selflessness by witnessing people sharing their last rupee or crumb of food so another may eat for that day.
- I learned I could listen to my innate knowledge, which protected me when I feared for my life in Kashmir.
- I learned I could be in service, which led me to teach English

to a Tibetan monk and let him teach me about friendship.
* And I learned that I could trust the voice within, which gave
me the courage to even ask for a private audience with the
Dalai Lama, and then—with the help of God, my dad, the
spirit world, my stubborn attitude, whatever you want to
call it—granted me those four unforgettable, life-changing
minutes.

My story is the quintessential tale of the power of intuition. Intuition
works when you can be present enough to hear a calling, feel it in your
body, and adhere to its message, even though you may not know the
outcome. Trust that you need to go where you need to go, that you need
to do what you need to do, and that this mystical message has your best
interests in mind.

My trip to India was a journey of destiny from a source beyond. I
was meant to land on Netflix that day at that time to watch that film.
I was fated to not travel for my fortieth birthday and instead stay and
heal my broken heart over the death of my father, and to travel a year
later and be blessed not only to meet His Holiness the Dalai Lama but
to face my grief and heal my soul, too. I want you to learn from my
journey that we don't always know the future; we can only believe in
the present. When you hear the call of fate, and the voice of intuition,
you listen, believe, and trust that there are forces outside your control
that are leading you to a better place. My place was India.

CHAPTER 5

All human knowledge begins with intuitions, proceeds from thence to concepts, and ends with ideas.

—*Immanuel Kant*

Your intuitive intelligence, like your skin and bones, is with you all the time. It is what gives humans the same instinctual behaviors. Watch someone when they hold a baby; they will naturally rock it back and forth. Similarly, when most people are on a plane and it is landing, they will turn to look out the window. Your intuition is with you and not going anywhere, and all you need to do to find a healthier lifestyle is tap into its wisdom. Try to remember that you have this secret vault of wisdom with you all the time, and when you are struggling, get out your keys and open it for support.

Just as you intuitively remember certain behaviors, you may also be prone to forget things. Because it is easy to live on autopilot, doing and saying all the same things out of habit, you may fail to remember that intuition is a built-in radar you can connect to for advice. The more you practice connecting to it, the more powerful it becomes. Think about it.

If you play the piano every day, you will become a more prolific pianist; if you made it a habit to speak French every day, you would eventually speak it more fluently. Intuition works the same way.

We all know how important intuition is to our lives, but we too often forget it. So I want to share some tips for your intuitive toolbox. In this toolbox there are internal and external life skills, and activities that will help your body become healthier, your decision-making skills stronger, and your intuitive path clearer.

The Internal Toolbox

Your internal world revolves around your emotional states: falling in love, grieving the loss of a loved one, or feeling joy when you succeed at school, work, or parenting. These intuitive moments happen in a quiet way between you and your soul.

Be Present

The first step in accessing your internal world is to hear your intuition by becoming present. I know you have heard time and time again how important it is to be in the present moment, but that is because there is such a power in this message. There is a beautiful quote from the turtle character, Master Oogway, in the movie *Kung Fu Panda*. He tells Po, "You are too concerned about what was and what will be. There is a saying: 'Yesterday is history, tomorrow is a mystery, but today is a gift. That is why it is called the present.'"

Recognize that there are times when you may be moving at Mach speed. At this velocity it is impossible to see anything around you. To reach the present moment, simply get quiet, breathe in and out for three seconds, and bring your body into a restful state. In this peaceful place, ask your intuition the questions you are struggling with. Pay attention to the different sensations in your body—a pulling on your gut or a fluttering in your heart, signs that a deep cavern is opening within you, a cavern designed to echo your calling.

Being in the present moment may be uncomfortable, because you are forced to wake up to each and every moment as it is, not as you would wish it to be. But once you surrender and accept your situation, the world stops and your intuition becomes clear as a bell.

I remember watching *Jeopardy!* in the hospital with my father when he was sick. "This sucks; I am in a hospital room," I remember thinking, "with machines beeping, having to see my father paralyzed and sitting in his wheelchair." But then I turned from the TV and saw my father smiling, and I realized that even though I'd rather be with him anywhere but a hospital room, I needed to embrace this precious moment, because it may never come again, and it didn't—he died six months later.

By being present, the same way I was in that hospital room, and by accepting whatever arises, you can embrace each miracle around you, too.

Follow the Intuitive Voice

After becoming more present, the next tool to pull out of your toolbox is to follow the intuitive voice you hear. But how can you distinguish between which voice is your intuition, sent from the deepest parts of your soul to guide you toward a more fruitful life, and which is your inner critic or judging mind? Start by asking yourself, "Do I feel good or bad when I hear this voice?" and "Does it make me feel inspired or full of shame?" Then, once you recognize your intuitive voice, listen deeply to it, and follow it. You may hear, "Quit your job," "Fight for your marriage," or "Go to India."

Whatever you hear, you must not be afraid—do not let fear drive your actions. You must ask yourself, "Is there a lesson I need to learn?" and "Is there a journey I need to travel?" and "Is there a gift I need to receive?" One of my favorite hymns in Catholic Mass, "Be Not Afraid," gives me courage. The lyrics are "Be not afraid. I go before you always. Come follow me, and I will give you rest. If you pass through raging waters in the sea, you shall not drown. If you walk amid the burning flames, you shall not be harmed. . . . Know that I am with you through it all." When I face my fears, I can trust that when I am called to go on a journey, I can go and I will be protected. It is about trust; it can be scary to follow a voice that is in your soul, but also transformative.

Surrender to What Life Is Teaching You

The final tool to strengthen your intuition is to surrender to what life is teaching you. Try to accept all the emotions and circumstances that come your way, the ones that make you feel good, safe, or comfortable *and* the dark ones—grief, loss, rage, anger, jealousy, or sadness.

We tend to push the dark so far away, but "one does not become enlightened by imagining figures of light," Swiss psychotherapist Carl Jung said, "but by making the darkness conscious." Consider what happens in the dark: We make love in the dark. Babies are formed in the dark womb. The stars come out in the dark, and fireworks are more vibrant in the dark. Most plants, fruits, and vegetables are grown in rich, dark soil. When you wake up in the middle of the dark night, if you listen closely you may hear the voices of your ancestors, spirits, and guides. They say the spiritual world is the most permeable and the veils the thinnest in the middle of the night. The spirits come out to play and give us messages to help us learn and grow and transform ourselves. Remember as a child running around your neighborhood playing flashlight tag or catching fireflies as the sun set and the darkness arrived. It was this beautiful combination of being scared, yet fully alive and awake, as if all your senses were heightened, and it all happened in the dark.

The dark burns away the superficial. It burns away the past and future, too, leaving only the present. Our bodies and minds quiet down in the dark, so our hearts and spirits can open up to receive, heal, replenish, refresh, and be reborn. When we are in our dark—with our sadness, grief, anxiety, depression, or jealousy—we can tell our deepest truths and see our true selves, at our rawest yet most beautiful.

The next time you face a dark situation, ask yourself, "Can I surrender and embrace each emotion as it arises? Can I resist the urge to fight my circumstances or try to control the outcome? Can I surrender to my situation and let the natural rise and fall of life come my way?"

A simple yet typical example of facing darkness happens in the light of day when we hit a traffic jam. You will most likely feel frustrated and annoyed and will question your life choices. "Why do I live in a place with a two-hour commute? What am I doing spending most of my life in my car?" At this moment, surrender and let this annoyance teach you patience, let these questions dive you deeper into your life choices, and don't shy away from your dark emotions. Sometimes our intuition shines the brightest in our darkest moments.

When you embrace your dark emotions and practice life with curiosity instead of rigidity, your intuitive voice will embrace those emotions as well, turning negative situations into positive ones. When you embrace your darkness without going into suffering, you will transform. The intuitive voice may sound different, it may be barely audible, but it is there. It may sound like "Get a new job. Move to a smaller town without traffic." Or it may say, "You love your job, and this is part of embracing your career. Use this time to be quiet and meditate or listen to a podcast you have always wanted to and now have the time to. This is your opportunity to accept your emotions instead of despising them."

The External Toolbox

Think of being in a dense forest and not being able to see beyond the trees. Or walking the streets of New York City, with all its skyscrapers, and not being able to see the horizon. Your personal energy field can get blocked, too, leaving you unable to hear, see, or sense what your intuition is trying to tell you. How do you stay clear?

You start by combining your internal toolbox with external actions, three of them in particular: having a meditation practice, making your body a priority, and exercising.

Meditate

Meditation is one of the most powerful tools to heal anxiety, depression, addiction, ADD, and trauma, and it provides clearer access to one's intuition. "Dedicating some time to meditation is a meaningful expression of caring for yourself that can help you move through the mire of feeling unworthy of recovery," renowned Buddhist and meditation teacher Sharon Salzberg writes. "As your mind grows quieter and more spacious, you can begin to see self-defeating thought patterns for what they are, and open up to other, more positive options."

One of the easiest pathways to this peaceful state is to sit in silence, breathe, let go of your thought patterns, observe what comes up for you in a state of stillness, and notice what your mind does to clutter your pure self. Meditation can be challenging and super uncomfortable because you must sit and hear your judging and comparing mind. But by not running away from yourself, you can let go, build a more resilient mind, and clear away toxic thoughts to make more room for your heart.

Is this the only way to meditate? No.

Meditation can look like many different things. Life is busy. Allow yourself to meditate when you can—while you walk from your car to your office, wait for your kids to run out from school, or, don't laugh, but even when you are on the toilet. Yes, it's crazy but true: there are times when you are going to the bathroom, being forced to sit in one place, and you can just breathe and move whatever needs to move. Meditation is one of your spiritual gateways to growth, which you can access anytime you participate in an activity that takes you out of the endless chatter of the mind.

Nourish

Another external tool to deepen your intuition is to become more aware of what you put into your body. I love to indulge in most foods with friends and family. Food is one of my purest joys. I am not writing any of this claiming to be a diet guru. I have a coffee every day; I love pizza, and my sweet tooth is off the charts. Yet I am acutely aware of foods that affect my energy and distort my intuitive voice.

What you put into your body affects your emotional state. And if you want to enhance your intuitive voice, become aware of your diet and health. If you eat heavy foods all day, your body will feel heavy. It comes down to energy. Food is and carries energy. For example, if you eat a fresh salad, grown on an organic farm with loads of love and care, those vegetables will fill your body with healthy karmic energy. On the other hand, if you eat a frozen meal made in a factory from preservatives and additives, you are putting chemicals—not even real food—into your body, and you will clog up your spiritual channel with toxins and unhealthy energy, which will in turn keep your intuitive voice quieter.

Think about the foods and liquids you put into your body every day. Are they creating more clarity and energy, or are they forcing the body to have to fight with its natural chemistry? If you find yourself feeling bloated, tired, and unclear, this is the moment you can choose to treat your body with fresh juices, greens, fruit, and most importantly love.

As I write this I am eating a croissant and drinking a coffee, and I am so happy. One of the worst things you can do to your body is inhibit its intuitive voice by shaming it. When you consume a food or drink that may not be the best for you, try not to get mad at yourself or put yourself down. But admit that you may need to repair your body in order to help it function on a healthy spiritual level. Wake up to what you put in your body, and do it with love, acceptance, and care.

Exercise

Once you establish a meditation practice and become more aware of what you are putting in your body, you will naturally have more motivation to move. Make exercise a part of your life. Make it a priority in your weekly schedule. You do not have to summit Mount Everest or run a marathon. Listen with curiosity to your body and have your movement be about you and your preferences and interests, because that is what will sustain your practice. Your routine can be as simple as walking with a friend, doing some yoga when you wake up, running around the block, or taking a salsa dancing class.

When you give yourself the gift of exercise, you give yourself the gift of greater intuition, too. I was on a solo run in the woods when I heard the title for my first book, *Cracking Open*. I was on a hike in the mountains when I realized I wanted to have a second child. And it was in my weekly yoga class that I was able to grieve the loss of my father, reminding myself I would feel joy again. When you exercise, you are saying to your body, "I care so much about my physical and emotional well-being that I will give you thirty minutes to an hour of my precious attention." When you take care of your body, your body will take care of you—the essence of self-love.

Your body does better when relaxed, when your brain is in a resting state. When you are stressed, however, cortisol is pumping throughout your body. This hormone can create a fight-or-flight response, also called the acute-stress response. A fight-or-flight response disrupts the body's natural rhythm, which may cause headaches and struggles with breathing and put extra pressure on your heart. Your external toolbox—meditation, diet, and exercise—will help you avoid these flight-or-flight scenarios and, combined with your internal toolbox, will help you create a healthier internal state for decision making.

Using the Tools to Make a Change

I had a client who came to me because she was having the hardest time making decisions, big or small. It could be anything from "Should I switch my child's school?" to "Should I stay in my marriage?" She would worry about what other people might think, or what would happen if she made the wrong decision. Once she would commit to a decision, she would question it, so much so that it was causing her terrible anxiety, keeping her up at night, and keeping her from enjoying the company of others and pursuing her passions.

In our sessions we would discuss how to help her strengthen her intuition and decision-making powers. I would ask her, "What is inhibiting you from staying in the here and now?" and "Why are you letting other voices drown out your one true voice?" and "What would it feel like to be empowered while making your decisions?"

While staying curious, I would also suggest she try surrounding herself with people, places, and activities that would bring her back to her body and heart and free her from the chatter in her mind—attending a weekly meditation class, walking daily, or adding one green juice to her diet. We also talked about breathing, going to a yoga class, and spending time around the people who she felt loved and supported her. I know these things may sound quite simple, but they are quite hard. Changing our behavior can be very challenging; it takes dedication, drive, and a will for a better life.

After a month or so, she was not struggling as much with making her decisions. She changed her daughter's school and found it did not cause her as much doubt and fear. She felt more self-assured in herself and was therefore more confident in her marriage. By changing some of her patterns of behavior, she was strengthening her decision-making power and liberating herself from her worries and fears in order to follow her heart.

Whether you are deciding to take out the dishes or have sex with your partner, the idea is to not allow your mind to wonder, to stay in the moment. When you can hear all your voices—your critic; your judge and jury; your wise, compassionate, loving voices—you can decide which ones are worth listening to, because only you know what your soul really longs for.

Imagine you are at a crossroad in your life, where you need to make some tough decisions. How clear would your intuition be if you could stay in the present, follow your callings, and accept all the emotions that arise? How would your spirit respond to changes if you were practicing meditation, filling your body with loving foods, and moving to its natural rhythm? I think you know the answer.

My client knew these answers after implementing many, if not all, of these tips from her toolbox into her life. She, like you, valued her clairvoyant voice and therefore made it a priority to do things in her daily life to enhance its presence. She found a way to wake up and witness what life was going to throw her way, and with an open heart, courageous spirit, and drive to treat herself with love and care, she found a way to trust her decisions with conviction.

CHAPTER 6

Everyone who wills can hear the inner voice. It is within everyone.

—*Mahatma Gandhi*

Massive amounts of information fly at us every day, five times as much as we were exposed to thirty years ago. That is over 174 newspapers full of information per day, according to the *Telegraph*. And the level of actual noise in our environments is much higher, too—outdoors the cars, buses, honking, yelling, street vendors, children at the nearby park; indoors the dinging texts, ringing cell phones, and televisions everywhere we look. Everything seems to occur at one time, too: I've been washing the dishes while the phone rang, music played, and my children peppered me with questions. Sometimes I have no idea what they even ask me, let alone what the answer is.

We also have a plethora of voices in our heads: "Take out the garbage," "Pay that bill," "You need to exercise because you ate twenty cookies last night," or the inner critic that says, "You are a crummy parent because your kid was mean to another kid." That inner critic can be loud and can overtake us with stories that can torture us all day. I am sure you have been there, where something happens and you convince yourself that you did something wrong, or someone did something wrong to you. It is the inner critic talking, creating a false story and robbing you of joy.

With all this internal and external noise, no wonder we have a hard time hearing our one true intuitive voice.

Intuitive Guide: Jay

This journey of finding our true intuitive voice has led me to people who live on the beautiful island of Kauai in Hawaii, bustling New York City, remote hot springs, an island off the state of New Jersey, and serene Bozeman, Montana. Little did I know my next intuitive guide, who would teach us about distinguishing between all our voices, would be four blocks from my home in Bend, Oregon, at an old country store that was miraculously turned into a bustling restaurant. My family and I walk through their warm and loving doors every week for a great cup of coffee, phenomenal cheesy sticks, and pasta that is out of this world.

Today I am heading to this restaurant not to grab a salad or cardamom sea-salt latte, no; I am meeting the creator and owner, Jay. While I was in my research phase of writing, he kept popping into my mind as someone I may want to interview, not because his wife and sister are dear friends of mine—no, this reason was beyond friendship. Not because he has built a successful restaurant atmosphere—no, this choice was beyond good ingenuity. And not because he is a practicing Buddhist—no, this was beyond learning from his dedicated practice. He kept arriving in my field of vision because he is a recovering addict, and I wanted to inquire how intuition had played a part in his addiction and more importantly how it affects his years of sobriety. I want this book to be a healing tool for many, and according to a study conducted by the Substance Abuse and Mental Health Services Administration (SAMHSA), 23.5 million people are addicted to drugs or alcohol in the United States. Because of this, I felt it was very important to include addiction, and who else to ask than my recovering, successful, Buddhist friend Jay.

I walked in through the swinging front porch door and was greeted with a warm hug. We sat down, and he began sharing with me how intuition was at play when he opened the restaurant. He found the space and had an idea to open a farm-to-table restaurant, yet everyone around him said it would be impossible. There was not enough parking, they had said, and the lease payment was too high, and the economy had just tanked. But he chose to listen to the one voice that said yes, and the restaurant has been a success beyond his expectations. He hit a home run by staying present and listening to the voice that said, "This is possible," versus the voices that were saying, "This is impossible."

As he spoke, I found myself looking around the bustling restaurant and being reminded of his successful life as a husband, father, and restaurateur, yet knowing his life had not always been a home run.

Jay grew up in a Chicago suburb with his loving sister, full-time working mom, and creative dad. Jay's dad would often tell his mom he was taking Jay on a father-son outing, and then whisper to Jay as they were walking out the door, "We are going to go see the bat caves," local slang for the hometown bars. Because of his early introduction to alcohol, Jay was well acquainted with local town bars, which is why it is not surprising he picked up his first drink in sixth grade.

He was hooked and began walking down the slippery slope of experimenting with drugs. Once he found his love of cocaine, his life began to spiral in a way that most do around addiction. When he was twenty-five, he was arrested in Red Lodge, Montana, because he passed out at a stop sign with his foot on the gas. Lucky for Jay, someone filming his arrest captured one of the officers beating him up, therefore allowing his attorney to get all the charges dropped, and the addictive voice continued to rise.

The debauchery and denial did not stop there. Late one night in St. Croix, his drunken body was thrown out a Jeep's side door at forty miles an hour. The next thing he remembered was waking up on a beach with scabs all over his body, his clothes bloody. As he stumbled into town, he witnessed a man being beaten with a baseball bat. Hungover and in shock, Jay arrived at work two hours later in his blood-soaked shirt and asked for a drink.

His addiction began to bleed into his marriage and family as well. He would do a line of cocaine as his daughter slept in her crib, or take his kids out to the woods to hide his drinking from his wife, finding himself following in his father's footsteps. Sadly, Jay's addictive voice also began to tell him that he didn't love his wife anymore.

But it wasn't getting arrested, leaving his family, demolishing relationships, breaking bones, destroying his nasal passage from twenty years of cocaine use, or damaging his liver from over thirty years of drinking that got Jay sober. It was a quiet but intuitive voice that came late one evening after many hours of drinking and snorting cocaine. "You are really fucking lonely in this empty house," the voice said. "With no family, shades drawn, and totally high." Soon afterward he picked up the phone and called the addiction specialist who eventually got him sober.

As Jay shared these vulnerable and honest stories, I cautiously shoved a bite of eggs into my mouth before asking him how intuition played a role in his addiction and recovery—the topic I came to explore. A quiet, contemplative look ran across his face, a sign of his meditation practice at work.

"Intuition for me is about being in the present moment," he began after a moment of silence. "You see, when I am trying to make a decision on my intuition, I stop and become present in order to hear all the voices that are at play in this process. I don't just take one voice into account. The difficult thing is there are so many voices I am hearing, and if I don't stop and listen and recognize where are all these voices are coming from, I will not be able to know which one is my wise voice, or the voice of the trickster, the addict, or the voice of my parents. So if you are listening only for intuition, you are putting delusion in the way."

Jay paused for a moment. "When I was using drugs and alcohol, the voice of addiction was louder than any other voice, as illogical as that sounds. It would scream 'Use!' even after losing so much. The violence that surrounds that voice is amazing. Addiction taught me how to not take the first voice I hear at face value. I had to learn to decipher which voice was which, and for me this is the key to listening to my intuition—to stop, question, be present and patient in order to hear all the voices, and take time to find the wise one."

I am continually a student of life. Even though I am the author of this book, doing the interviews, research, and writing, I am the student in this moment. Jay is teaching each of us something that we may not always think about. Do we stop to become present and listen to all the voices? Or are we sometimes in a hurry and let our anxieties get in the way? Do we move too fast to escape our uncomfortable feelings? What Jay is speaking about is the need to sit in our bruised and battered self to find our one true voice.

Jay went on to tell me about hearing the voices that tell us we are a piece of shit and the voices that tell us we are better than others. The voices that scream, "Take a drink!" and the voices that say, "Go for a bike ride." Through his recovery he has also learned to hear the voice of his ego, the voice of wanting, the loud voice that says, "Be more, do more, and make more."

We all have this ego voice. To work with it, first recognize its language and how it speaks to you. It may sound like "I want to buy this house because it is bigger and better" or "I need to do this so that people feel like I am important and I am seen." The voice will sound like an "I" voice—I want, I need.

Once you identify this egoic voice, you will notice how it defines you and your persona for the outside world. "I am special because I was chosen for this award." Or "I am important because I have more money, am skinnier, or have a better spouse than you." You can see and decide how much you'd like to identify with that voice. You can go from "I will attend this event so people think I am special" to "I will not attend this event because I am tired and want to be home in my pajamas, eating ice cream." Which mind-set is your ego, and which is intuition from the heart?

The egoic voice and intuition, which is the voice of truth, are very different. The ego blinds our intuition and wants everything to be bigger or better. The ego is fear based, whereas intuition is surrounded by love. The ego is competitive and judgmental, whereas intuition is respectful and accepting. The intuitive voice will say, "You are evolving, and thank God, because this is how you learn to become the human being you are supposed to be."

"With all the voices that we hear every day," I asked Jay, "what gives us the ability to register which voices are our intuition, which voices are really the truth?"

"When you are listing to your intuition," he answered with confidence and ease, "not only do you have to decide between all the voices; you have to consider all the other emotions that are going on at the time you are making a certain decision. There was a time I was on a ten-day silent retreat and my body began to ache. Instead of taking the pain at face value, I followed the pain, listening for its wise voice. From the pain in my physical body, I began to hear the emotional pain that I carry in my body. I followed that emotion that led me to remembering the pain of seeing my father die."

Jay swallowed. "I was in the car with him as his tongue began falling out of his mouth, in the final phases of his life. You see, listening to your intuition is not a simple task. I could have simply heard, 'My body hurts,' but instead I opened up to the pain and was able to hear, 'No, my heart hurts because my dad died.' And that is the wisdom of intuition."

Can you see the beautiful teaching here? When you are in pain, be it physical or emotional, can you be brave enough to find its root cause, to ultimately face your grief? It could be the grief around the death of loved ones, or the grief of your growing children, or the grief of failed expectations. Whatever it may be, I've found that when people muster the courage to arrive here, they can look at the pain with an honest soul, then heal inside this space of truth.

Michael Singer talks about the concept of inner pain in his book *The Untethered Soul*:

> "Even though you may not actually like the feelings of inner disturbance, you must be able to sit quietly inside and face them if you want to see where they come from. Once you can face your disturbances, you will realize that there is a layer of pain seated deep in the core of your heart. This pain is so uncomfortable, so challenging, and so destructive to the individual self, that your entire life is spent avoiding it. Your entire personality is built upon ways of being, thinking, acting, and believing that were developed to avoid this pain."

By moving past your inner and outer pain, Singer seems to be saying, you can arrive at your intuition, where real growth happens.

"How do we have enough wisdom to let ourselves look at all our voices and determine which one is intuitively right for us now?" I asked Jay.

"First get really honest about what each voice is saying. I always believe the voice I am hearing is neither right or wrong. I don't believe the bullshit I am hearing. I question it and go deeper to find the voice of reason." He had to find this way of listening to his voice with duality because when he was in the throes of his addiction he listened only to the voice that said, "Keep drinking," and now he knows he cannot just believe one voice; he has to open himself up to get present and listen to all the voices. "That voice of addiction sounded real, and if I learned from my experience I know that any voice saying something to me may or may not be true. It could be energy, a feeling, our shadow, our inner critic." Realize how crucial it is to question and analyze this first intuitive voice and not immediately take it at face value, especially if you want to face your "stuff"—your emotional traumas—and grow.

After an hour enamored with Jay's insight, I got one more nugget of wisdom from him. "Basically what happens after years of practicing being present and not taking any of the voices we hear at face value, the negative voices begin to disappear. My voice around obsessing over using drugs and alcohol is basically gone. Not that I don't have any negative voices; it is just that I have learned to trust my intuitive wisdom as my compass for truth." He was quiet for a moment. "The daily intuitive voice I hear now, my deepest truth, is sobriety, family, meditation, and business."

And then I intuitively heard, "Thank you, Jay."

CHAPTER 7

LISTENING TO YOUR BODY'S INTUITIVE WISDOM

It's also helpful to realize that this very body that we have, that's sitting right here right now . . . with its aches and its pleasures . . . is exactly what we need to be fully human, fully awake, fully alive.

—Pema Chödrön

I have asked hundreds of people one question: "What does intuition mean to you?" Usually the first thing I hear is something like "Intuition is a feeling in my body. I may experience a strong pull in my heart, or my gut twists and turns." Or "My entire body told me this was the right or wrong decision." Or "When the phone rang, my whole body stiffened up and I just knew who was calling." Most people's first encounter with intuition is in the body. They experience a strong yearning, a pulling or stirring in their belly, or their palms sweat or hearts race.

"My heart was beating out of my chest." "My stomach was in knots." "I got cold feet." All terms coined because our bodies have a way of transmitting important information that originates in our souls. We have feelings throughout our organs and muscles that are unseen to the eye, sensations that are our bodies' intuitive way of turning up the volume so we will listen to what they need to tell us.

Bodily sensations broadcast themselves in many volumes. Sometimes they may come in loud, repeating a message that you cannot ignore—stomach pains so intense you are buckled over in pain, or debilitating headaches that you cannot escape. Or they may arrive quieter, like a soft whisper, where you just know something is not right because your body is physically and energetically off. Regardless of how your intuition arrives in the body, it is hard to deny that is present and that it should be listened to with reverence.

Practice Listening to Your Body

Imagine an important decision you have to make. Go to a quiet place, take three deep breaths, and ask your body the question you are struggling with. Wait, be patient, pay attention, and don't rush your body for an answer. Notice what your body is telling you physically and energetically. Is your heart beating fast? Are you hearing a voice? Are you feeling a tug in your belly that gives you a sense of which direction you should take? When you hear the answers, let your body know that you trust its wisdom and deem it valid.

What can be confusing is that fear causes these same body sensations. And so often you may conduct your life from the cerebral part of your body, your brain, which makes it even more challenging to get in touch with your gut feelings. So how do you discern between fear and intuition?

The first sign it's intuition and not fear is that you feel present. Let's practice. Ask yourself, "What should I do right now?" Listen. What did you hear? Did you hear to keep reading, go to the bathroom, or get a glass of water? That is your intuition talking from the present moment you are in, right now. Or you may have heard, "I am lazy for spending time reading a book. I need to get up and do the laundry." Or "Shoot,

I forgot to call this person back. I need to do it now." These words are coming from a place of shame and guilt; they are coming from your fears.

The second sign is when your emotions are neutral, when you are prepared to make decisions based on how you feel right now, not from a place of regret about the past or worry about the future. Fear is emotionally charged. It has energy of anxiety, darkness, and ambiguity, so your body may speak the language of fear: a restless stomach, for instance, or a racing heart. But when you will not waver on a decision—when it feels right, calm, and affirming—that's intuition talking.

I remember the day I decided to travel to India. I had some concerns, but I was not afraid or anxious. I felt present, grounded, and secure in my decision to go abroad. That was my intuition. I also remember the day I accepted a job that I knew was not in my best interests. I felt sick to my stomach, and my heart was racing. That was fear.

When you don't know whether you are deciding from a place of fear or intuition, ask yourself these questions: "How do I feel when I am with this person or in that situation?" "When I imagine myself at this new job or in this new house or city, what do I feel in my body?" "Why am I experiencing these emotions?"

You don't find the roots of a tree unless you go deeper into the earth. By digging a bit deeper into your body's experiences, you will discover more of your truth. Let your body be your greatest teacher.

Intuitive Guide: Trisha Coburn

I wanted to find a pertinent example of how listening to our bodies' internal wisdom helps us make decisions, and I found the perfect one in an *O, The Oprah Magazine* article about five women whose hunches changed their lives. Trisha Coburn was one of those women, and her story—about a premonition that literally saved her life—stood out as an incredible feat of intuition. I emailed asking if

I could interview her, she kindly said yes, and we set a date to talk on the phone.

At forty-six years old, Trisha began having eerie dreams that left her with feelings she could not forget. She told me how in the first dream she saw herself witnessing the Holocaust. She stood behind a barbed-wire fence across from six ghostly-looking people with white, gaunt faces, dark circles around their eyes, Xs over their mouths. They were on their knees begging her to do something in a language Trisha could not understand. She awoke shaken and distraught.

The same dream came again with more than a dozen people attempting to communicate with her about something she knew she needed to listen to. A week later the dream returned. Now there were over twenty people begging her. She awoke sobbing and was unable to fall back asleep.

Trisha knew something was not right in her body and made an appointment with her doctor. "There is a very thin line between our awareness and the spiritual side," Trisha said. "It is like a film you can press on, yet we have to be willing to live in conscious faith and be open to listening to our dreams and body to have access to its awareness." Even though her doctor thought she was overreacting, she convinced him to do blood work. When the results came back fine, she could breathe a sigh of relief and stop worrying that these dreams were some message about her own health.

A week later, the dream came back, and this time there were over a hundred people wailing and pleading with her. "I don't know what you want from me!" she screamed back. "Please, please tell me what I am supposed to do!" Yet no message was received.

A few days later came her fifth and final dream. Trisha was back at the fence, and nobody was there. She fell to her knees, sobbing. "Come back. I need you to help me." And out of nowhere she heard a voice in clear English say, "Look deeper."

Trisha returned to her doctor and inquired where the deepest part of the body is. He told her it was the colon. Even though insurance would not cover a colonoscopy because she was under fifty, she went ahead and found one of the best doctors in New York City to perform this often painful procedure.

Trisha is an artist and a visual person and couldn't resist the opportunity to stay awake during the procedure and witness what was occurring in her body. She sat uncomfortably as the scope maneuvered its way through the colon, when all of a sudden there it was: a black mass, a tumor. "Oh my, you must have a guardian angel," the doctor said.

"Or I have hundreds," Trisha thought.

Trisha's cancer was aggressive and fast moving, but because she listened to her eerie dreams and her body, she is cancer free today.

"There is more wisdom in your body than in your deepest philosophies," Friedrich Nietzsche said. The body is such an incredible vehicle to teach us what we need to know and need to obtain. If you trust its intuitive nature, you will form a deeper relationship to your whole self—and you could even save your life.

We are programmed to listen to other people's opinions about our bodies and to rely solely on concrete experiences—certainly not dreams—for wisdom. How many times have you not felt quite right but heard "Oh, I am sure you are fine; you are just stressed, or tired" or "Don't make a mountain out of a molehill"? Trisha heard this advice as well, but thankfully she has a strong sixth sense, so she trusted her dreams.

Since Tricia was a child, she always seemed to know when or when not to spend time with people, or if she was in danger. She had a challenging childhood and learned at an early age to rely on her intuition to heal. "So much of our illnesses come from childhood trauma," she said. "The body holds trauma around emotional, psychological, and sexual abuse."

As a therapist, I could not agree more. Sadly, some level of trauma occurs to most children—anything from being bullied at school to being abused at home. It is awful, painful, and a travesty to the child-like spirit. Trauma clogs your body, just as soap scum clogs a drain, and this blockage makes it harder to feel or hear your intuition. Children then learn to question their sixth sense and bodily wisdom and carry this distrust throughout their adult lives.

Trisha's traumatic childhood played a part in her dismissal of her intuition. As an adult she found herself in relationships where she did not trust herself, and she learned a valuable life lesson: it is much harder to listen to your intuition when you are not in healthy situations. "There have been times where I felt like a part of me was tucked away," Trisha said. "But by following my intuition, I am back full force, ready to hear my soul's work and not be afraid to trust my inner wisdom. It's about trust. It's been a journey."

Toward the end of our conversation, we talked about fear and intuition. "Don't be afraid of intuition," Trisha said. "Fear is just a way of self-doubting and talking yourself out of things." I couldn't agree more. We have become afraid to trust the inner wisdom of our bodies. We run away from its voices out of fear of the unknown. To heal we must face our fears, befriend our bodies, and open ourselves up to greater health and well-being. Nourish your body emotionally and spiritually with love, educate yourself with expert advice, visit practitioners you admire and respect, and, above all, trust your inner wisdom—you know a lot more about your own body than you realize.

Your body is the first voice you should listen to when you wake up in the morning and, if you aren't afraid to listen to your lucid dreams, when you go to sleep at night. Nor should you be afraid to listen to your internal wisdom or to wonder whether a new bodily sensation may be the symptom of something harmful. As the famous dancer Martha Graham said, "The body never lies."

On days when Trisha is afraid and distraught, she has a voice that tells her, "What you need is right here in front of you." We talked about how it takes immense courage to be shown what you need to see, and then to truly look at it. This is the key; we all have the power of intuition, but can we all wake up and have the strength to follow its voice once we hear what it has to say?

I am going to wake up, listen, and take this advice to heart. Trisha has spent her life listening to her intuition around her body, life, and career. And from this deep place of knowing, Trisha is alive today to share her wisdom and knowledge for us all to learn. By listening to your body, you may open your dream business, leave an unhealthy relationship, or even save your life. Can you wake up today to make your intuitive body sensations a part of your decision-making process? Is it possible to make interpreting your body's signs and signals a driving force in your life? "I sing the body electric," Walt Whitman said. Let your body be your electric force and embrace all that life brings your way.

CHAPTER 8

We are all visitors to this time, this place. We are just passing through. Our purpose here is to observe, to learn, to grow, to love . . . and then we return home.

—*Australian Aboriginal proverb*

Have you ever watched children in a religious setting or community activity? They don't question if the pastor, shaman, or bandleader asks them to come to the front of the church or stage to dance or sing or perform some other ritual. They usually run as fast as they can to participate. They are simply following their intuition; all that matters to them is the present moment.

Ritual is a natural rhythm of life, which is why it feels so intuitive, and why *Homo sapiens* have for thousands of years been performing acts of worship or sacrament, recognizing rites of passage, taking oaths of allegiance, and participating in ceremonies that help us access our deepest unconscious, connect to our higher selves, and open up our intuitive portals to nourish, heal, and transform our bodies and souls. Blowing out candles to celebrate a birthday, greeting someone by shaking their hand, dancing and toasting at a wedding—each a modern-day performance steeped in ancient ritual. Whatever they look like, all rituals share a similar purpose: to help humans transition from one life stage to another.

We all have some sort of ritual. The Dalai Lama wakes up at 3:00 a.m. to meditate, and the rock star Alice Cooper watches kung fu movies and eats Skittles before every show. Your ritual may be attending church to be alone with your god, surfing among the spiritual sea life and the majestic ocean, walking a labyrinth, or riding for miles on your bike. Or it could be more communal: a weekly gathering of friends over a cup of tea or a glass of wine, for instance, where you discuss family, career, or a book, or laugh about how you said something inappropriate at a meeting, or cry about your daughter struggling at college. Or a gathering of like-minded people passionate about a certain cause—the environment, human rights, marriage equality, or neighborhood safety. The individuals in these ritual communities support one another in a world of war and weapons while simultaneously uplifting one another with stories of people who have faced travesties with courage and grace. Wherever you land, your ritual community is healing and supportive, and when you leave these gatherings, you feel better than you did when you arrived.

If your ritual practice goes against the status quo, family dogma, or cultural norm, however, you may collide with others' opinions and make them uncomfortable. They may question your actions, judge you, or issue fearful words about your choices. But you must stay strong in your beliefs, knowing your practice is healing and therefore helping you stay healthy, intuitive, and happier for your family and friends.

Your ritual practice may even make you uncomfortable, too. In ritual you usually face your own shadow—the dark parts of your personality, your jealousy and rage, your insecurities. Ritual gives you a flashlight to examine these most shameful parts of your unconscious in order to heal. When you look at your dark sides closely, they do not have as much power over you. Think of a dark, damp cave: the deeper you go into the darkness, the more beautiful, mysterious, and interesting the cave becomes. The crystalized stalagmites can only grow in the darkest parts of the cave. Your psyche is the same way: the deeper you go, the richer you become. Ritual is your cave to grow deeper into your intuition.

I learned more about this cave while writing *Trust Within*. A dear friend generously opened her home in Ojai, California, so that I would have some space to write. On this personal writer's retreat I intuitively knew how necessary it would be to talk about ritual's important role in more deeply accessing your intuition. While in Ojai I was introduced to a magical place called Meditation Mount, up in the mountains high above the orange orchards and among a valley of rolling hills. It is truly heaven on earth. In one of my thirty-minute meditations up on the mountain one morning, I felt a deep connection to ritual, the impact it has had on my own intuition, and the importance it has played in my life.

My Relationship to Ritual

I have had the great fortune of engaging in ritual my entire life. I was raised in a dedicated and loving Catholic family where ritual was important. My first memory of ritual was when I was about four or five. I was at Saint Joan of Arc Church, sliding back and forth on a wooden pew, with the sweet smell of incense in the air and the booming, vibrating pipes of the organ filling the church with music. All my senses—sight, smell, sound, feel, and intuition—were fully awake. I was intuitively aware that in this sacred space I felt more connected to God and the divine part of myself. Since that day I have committed to my ritual practice, which has transformed to include more than just Mass, but also my meditation and yoga practice, travels around the world, and gatherings with other seekers at a dinner table, campfire, or church basement, all in hopes to reflect and discuss topics with authenticity, vulnerability, and a desire to heal.

Yet I have learned my greatest teachings with my ceremonial community. We participate in a tradition from Brazil called the Santo Daime, where people come together, wear white, and connect to other worlds and spirits for deep healing of the soul. When I first heard of this ritual, my judging mind was roaring: "That is so weird. Who would ever do that? I would never participate in something like that, ever." I realized I was judging this ancient tradition because I was scared, but my intuition was not scared. I kept hearing my little voice whispering, "This is for you. Do not be afraid." And it was not only whispering; it was not going away. One day I mustered up the courage to participate in this ritual of healing, surrendering, prayer, and transformation. There is no science that can prove why this ritual—with its community in a circle, singing, praying, and dancing all for the benefit of physical and emotional purging—heals. But it works for me; I am less anxious, more heart-centered, less judgmental, and so much more open-minded. I am a more patient parent, a more available spouse; I can face my challenges with less drama and a more compassionate soul. I am definitely more intuitive. And more than anything I am so grateful for the Santo Daime and its loving, accepting, openhearted community, where I can fully connect to myself.

It does not matter where you engage in ritual—alone or with a community, every day or once a year. What is important is opening yourself to the experience and noticing the healing that occurs. Only then can you walk your path with more intuition, guidance, and grace and heal your own wounds in order to heal the wounds of others. In that sense, ritual is about an individual experience within a collective community to create a universal healing.

Chakra Meditation

Chakras are seven energetic centers in your body in which energy flows. They are located in the base of the spine, lower abdomen, upper abdomen, heart, throat, forehead between the eyes—your "third eye"—and on the top of your head. They each represent a different color and physical, emotional, and spiritual states of being, such as stability, creativity, personal power, verbal expression, intuition, and living in your highest power. Chakra meditation helps to clear away any stuck energy or trauma held in the body and the chakra centers.

I have led hundreds through this ritual, and it helps them feel lighter and discover a clearer path to their deepest insights. To connect to your chakras, first sit quietly, close your eyes, and take three deep breaths. As you breathe, I want you to imagine that your fears, anxieties, and concerns are being washed away and you are filling your whole body with peace. Now I want you to imagine a beautiful white, gold, or rose light coming into your body. This light will enter the top of your head, which is your crown chakra, and begin to travel throughout all your chakra centers and body. Let this light move down the energetic channels of the chakras, enter your physical body of cells and nerves, bones and tendons. Allow this healing light to infuse every organ, your liver, pancreas, gallbladder, heart. As the light enters each organ—your heart in particular—let it swirl around and release any toxins stored there; let it heal any past traumas, current confrontations, or future worries. Some organs will need more time with the light than others; let that happen.

After your energetic and physical bodies have received all the light they need, take three deep breaths to come back to your present moment. Slowly open your eyes, and allow yourself to come back into the room. Does your body feel different? Do you feel a bit lighter, clearer, and less worried? Do you have a sense of optimism and encouragement to go back out into the world? Do you feel like you could make some decisions from a place of ease and confidence? Do you feel more open to connect with your intuition? Do you feel you've begun to clear away the things that don't serve you anymore—anxieties, fears, ego—in order to hear your true callings?

Ritual as Ancient Wisdom

When you participate in a ritual, you are tapping into the ancient wisdom that everything you need is already deep inside you.

The San people of Botswana at the Mountain of the Gods in the Kalahari Desert knew of this wisdom and practiced its rituals for seventy thousand years. They may have been in a cave, with arrowheads and a different language, whereas we are participating in a living room with a yoga mat, a rosary at Mass, or glass of wine at a book club, but it does not matter because we are both attempting to accomplish the same outcome. We are yearning for a spiritual ceremony to create a place for our feelings, a container to hold all our sadness and joys. Ritual is your right; you deserve to find a spiritual community where you can dive down deep into your well of wisdom and let go of any useless worry or shame you are carrying, connect with yourself and others, and find a clearer passage to your profound intuition.

CHAPTER 9

KEEPING CHILDREN'S INTUITION ALIVE

Don't try to comprehend with your mind. Your minds are very limited. Use your intuition.

—Madeleine L'Engle

One dark morning I blurrily saw a photo on the front page of the *New York Times*: a five-year-old Syrian boy, his fragile body covered in old ripped clothes, his doll-like face splattered with dust, mud, and encrusted blood. The caption read, "Omran Daqneesh, 5, was rescued after an airstrike in the Syrian city of Aleppo." I had to rub my sleepy eyes to make sure the photo was real. This innocent child, who should have been out playing freely in nature, was sitting alone in a bright-red chair, legs dangling above the floor, at a local aid station. He stared into space with look of shock, his face telling the story of Syria's immense trauma, loss of innocence, and the reality of the destruction their country has endured.

As odd as this may sound, I sensed that this young child, who had been through more in his short five years than most of us will go through in our entire lives, was somehow still whole. I felt in my bones—the bombs, destruction, and political strife did not destroy his sixth sense. By looking in his wise eyes, I could see that he knew the difference between right and wrong, that he carried the strength of a warrior, and that he knew deep down that even though his body had been through war, his spirit was still alive. Something inside told me that this young child from an embattled, rebel-held part of Aleppo still had his intuition intact.

Even though I could feel this sweet boy was strong, I was still screaming inside: "This is wrong! How could this happen? What can I do?" As an adult, I was angry and I had a primal instinct to protect this child, a stranger who lived thousands of miles away. My gut reaction was to run to Syria and help in any way I could.

Seeing this unforgettable photo—the perfect representation of what we do not want for our children—was a wake-up call not only to the war in Syria, but also to the importance of preserving the innocence and intuition of children all over the world. If we open our eyes, we will see that as human beings we are naturally pulled toward supporting a child's spirit so that it can thrive. We wish for them to be joyful, happy, smiling, with uninhibited freedom from worry and pain, and we all want to keep our children's colorful imagination pure and alive. With a fire in my belly, I was reminded of a very important lesson: while we are on this planet, we have a job to do for all children, and that is to keep their intuitive souls alive.

The Innate Intuition of Children

Children come into the world with playful spirits and open intuitive channels. Newborn babies will cry uninhibited because they are hungry, wet, tired, or hurt. They don't worry if something is right or wrong; they follow their intuitive emotional barometer. This sixth sense continues as they grow. We have all watched children do exactly what they want, when they want to do it. They will choose to play with children whom they feel energetically connected to, and entertain their curiosities despite any dogma or parental or societal expectations. If they love to write, they will write with a stick in the dirt. If architecture is in their soul, they will build forts. If they are drawn to art, they will paint with their fingers on paper without a care in the world. They don't go through the monkey mind we do as adults, questioning every action and decision; "If I do this, will my parents be proud of me, will I be judged, or will people think I am weird?" No, generally a child's spirit will fly to wherever the winds of their passions blow it. And as adults one of the best things we can do for a child's intuitive spirit is to simply support its journey so it can soar.

I learned so much about a child's intuition at my first teaching job. It was in a small town, in the middle of the woods. It was a hodgepodge of levels educationally, emotionally, and physically. I taught twelve first, second, and third graders combined and had first graders who were reading and third graders who were not.

I had one student I will never forget. Her name was Mary, and she had Williams syndrome, a genetic disease present at birth. Although children with Williams syndrome face many challenges, they also tend to be social, friendly, and endearing. Mary was all these three and more. She warmed every heart she encountered; she followed her intuition at any cost. When she wanted or needed something, she made sure she got it.

One day in class we were studying similes, and I was sharing examples such as "You are as sweet as pie" and "You are as colorful as crayons." When it was time for the students to share an example of a simile, Mary wildly waved her hand. I called on her, and she stood up and said, "I have the best example. It is Miss Rowen"—my maiden name—"is as beautiful as Martin Luther King Jr." The other students were silent, likely in shock, while I began laughing hysterically. Laughing out of joy for her creativity, intuitive spirit, and unique use of similes. Laughing at the way she could see that my Irish white skin could be as beautiful as Martin Luther King's dark skin. What better example of a child in their intuitive soul, brave and uninhibited by the rules of silence we create in our society? This is why we need to keep our children as pure and grounded as possible.

Fostering a Child's Intuition

To help children's intuition grow, ask yourself these questions:

- How can I preserve, harness, and protect a child's interior world of intuition, dreams, creativity, and play?
- How can I support their physical, mental, and spiritual well-being so they can make the best decisions for themselves?

As a parent, educator, and child therapist, I have had the pleasure of a bird's-eye view into the beautiful inner world of children. Through my personal and professional life, I have discovered a few foundational tips and tools that can help keep a child's spirit free, so that they can continue to roll on the floor with unending laughter and stay fearless, goofy, and honest.

Your first job is to let children know that their intuition is real, that when they speak about their imagination and clairvoyance you believe them. You not only believe them; you value their inner guidance system and stay curious about what lives in their hearts.

Encourage their world of imagery by letting them know that you are interested in learning about everything they are seeing and hearing. If they tell you they see a polka-dot giraffe over in the corner, singing and dancing, play along. Ask the child, "What else is the giraffe doing? Should we invite it to play? Can we sing along with the polka-dot giraffe?" Keep this imagery going as long as you can. The deeper they go into their fantasies, the deeper they will develop their intuition.

When they share that they hear bells, whistles, or voices near and far, try to notice if you pop out of your childlike spirit and enter your adult-world mind of "That is not possible," "This is stupid," or "I don't have time for this." Just breathe and remember that your goal is to strengthen their tools of intuition. Only when they feel you believe them will they begin to share with you everything they see and hear.

Imagine a time in your life where you saw everything as it was, when nothing stood in your way. The image that comes to my mind is the first time I walked out to the rim of the majestic Grand Canyon. I saw all the vibrant red, orange, pink, and yellow. I felt the energy of years of humans traveling on its rocks, rivers, and rim. And I heard about the stories that the ancient voyagers who first discovered this land had told, and heard tales from modern-day tourists, too. I was fully present to feel, hear, and witness all that was around me. I was like a child in a candy store—I could not get enough.

This is intuition for children; this is how they walk through the world. They are fully alive, open, and receptive to the beauty of life. I would have been devastated if someone told me, "Oh, that is just your imagination. What you experienced at the Grand Canyon was not real." Children's intuitive worlds are very real, and when you support their imagination, they will feel freer and have the courage to follow their hearts.

Your second job as an adult helping children's intuition grow is to recognize that they can trust their body sensations, which will help them strengthen their gut instincts. Remember, our bodies are some of our greatest tools for intuition. Children feel things deeply, even more so than adults, and the more we encourage them to trust their body, the more they'll develop the wisdom to trust its sensations.

It is important to believe a child's psychic pain, too. Think back to when you were a child and you said to an adult, "In my heart I don't feel quite right about this or that person," or "I don't want to go here or there." In your body you felt something was not right. The adults in your life may have said, "Oh, honey, that is only in your imagination. You are fine. Nothing is wrong."

These words form a plaque in children's energetic channels and teach them to not listen to their intuition, avoid their bodily messages, and ignore one of their greatest systems for caution. Children then create ways to distrust their sixth sense and bodily wisdom.

I have told my children these words myself. As adults we mean no harm; we have all been programmed to live a certain way. As we grow older, we are presented with more fears and obligations that force us to live in our left brain and not trust what our body is trying to tell us. But by acknowledging when you say these words or when you discount a child's emotional ailments, you awaken yourself to what needs to change to keep a child's intuition alive. And by learning and trusting your own gut instincts, you are energetically transforming the too-common misconception that intuition is not real.

Lastly, I encourage you to have children ask themselves the big questions: "Who am I?" and "What is my purpose on earth?" and "Why am I here?" Pondering these questions will keep a child's creativity, inspiration, drive, curiosity, and self-awareness open. The big life questions are the soil that helps their intuitive seeds grow.

As the adult in their life, you should ask them big life questions as well: "What did you dream last night?" "How did that person, friend, coach, or teacher make you feel?" "Where do you feel the most alive?" Children are sponges waiting to absorb anything and everything. They are pure light; they come into the world with hearts and minds as expansive as the Milky Way. By encouraging them to be inquisitive, you will help them go into the wilderness of their intuition to discover more of themselves, and they will return with a clearer sense of what they hear, see, and feel in their body.

To preserve a child's intuitive journey, we must give them tools for when they experience trauma, stress, or fear. With their intuitive voices they can find their center of peace and have a well to dip into when they are lost, confused, scared, excited, or searching for creativity and inspiration. In this sacred center of peace they will find reassurance that it will all be okay. A child's ESP is their compass of truth; they rely on it to tell them whom to trust. If we can instill in children the confidence to trust their intuition, they will more likely be able to sense danger and react accordingly.

How do you teach children to trust their intuition in times of danger? You show them. If you are walking down the street with a child, for instance, and you sense danger, act accordingly. Cross the street and walk on the other side, or turn around and walk the other direction. After modeling this behavior, discuss with the child why you acted this way, without instilling fear. Say things such as, "I turned around because I felt something strong in my body tell me that we should not walk that way, and I listened to my inner wisdom." Or ask the child, "Have you ever felt uneasy about a person or a place? Well, I just did, and I trusted my intuitive wisdom." Tell them their intuition can lead them to wonderful experiences, and it can also keep them safe. This modeling of behavior followed by a conversation installs a deeper sense of support and wisdom in children.

When children feel that adults support and believe them, they can become more independent, better discern right from wrong, and stand up for what they believe in, which will give them strength and courage when faced with adversity. By trusting their intuition they will become more resilient, knowing that if they want to leave an uncomfortable situation, they can. With your support and their growing intuition, they'll be fully equipped to make the best choices.

Intuitive Guide: A Child's Wisdom

I treated a child who came in complaining about stomachaches. He would wake up and get ready for school with an ache in his belly that made him very uncomfortable most of the morning. His mother had done everything to help him—she took him to the doctor, changed his diet, gave him teas and tinctures—but nothing worked, and the stomachaches persisted.

I encouraged him to get quiet and lightly put his hand on his stomach. I then guided him to ask his stomach, "Why are you hurting?" He slightly squiggled in his chair, a bit uncomfortable with this new exercise. He was quiet for a few seconds but then shared, "My stomach hurts because I am scared."

"Why are you scared?" I asked.

"There is a boy at recess that is not nice to me," he said, quietly but clearly. "And I am scared to go to school."

I told him I was so sorry this was happening to him and now that we knew why his stomach was hurting, his parents and I could help him feel better.

This sweet boy was afraid to tell anyone, because he did not want to get the other boy in trouble. He kept his emotional pain inside until it started to affect him physically. This is what is so amazing about the body. It will speak, and if we listen to its voices, we can heal challenging situations. It is fascinating how when we have a physical ailment, such as a broken bone, the medical attention is immediate; we go to the doctor, get a cast, rest, and get taken care of. But if we have emotional or psychic pain, it is so much more difficult to ask for support, or to put on a "cast" to heal our inner pain.

Children carry so much joy and ignite a room when they walk in. Their pure spirits remind us why we exist. We all unconsciously do our spiritual work so that children can have a better place to live and play. "You are the bows from which your children as living arrows are sent forth," Lebanese artist and writer Kahlil Gibran said. One of your most important jobs is to give them tools to reach for in times of need.

Remember how I intuitively reacted when I saw Omran's sweet face? I felt a deep love for that child. His suffering reminded me of the importance not only of love, but of fostering a child's intuition so that he or she can continue to feel love. And fostering that intuition is about so much more than giving one child a better life; it is about helping human beings everywhere, because no matter where we live, how old we are, or what language we speak, we are all spiritual beings tethered together by love and intuition— the core of our being. We are not separate. We are one—one planet, one human race. So when we see one human being suffer, we all suffer.

When we help children access their intuition and love themselves, we help them tap into this grand spiritual network and develop a sense of self way more powerful than any Russian or Syrian bomb.

CHAPTER 10

EXPLORING THE RISKS OF IGNORING INTUITION

Sometimes you hear a voice through the door calling you.... This turning toward what you deeply love saves you.

—*Rumi*

Have you ever met someone and all of a sudden experienced an odd, almost scary feeling? Or entered a house and instantly felt shivers running through your body? Maybe you walked into a restaurant or store and knew you wanted to leave but didn't know why.

These feelings may come into the body as a chill hitting the top of your spine and racing down your back like a crack on the surface of a frozen lake. It may feel like the hairs on the back of your neck or arms are standing straight up, as if they are soldiers waiting for their admiral's command. Or you may feel as if you have a pit in the center of your belly growing as deep as the Grand Canyon.

These unpleasant, often confusing sensations shock and chill you to the bone, so much so that you don't even know what to make of them, and because they are not easily explained, they are hard to trust. But this sixth sense—this premonition of darkness—is one of our greatest teachers. It is our bodies warning us of dangers to come.

Sometimes we listen and react accordingly. We may look around, scan our environment, or take note of the person we felt this darkness radiate from, and trust our intuition's antennae to point us where we need to go. Other times we may ignore its voice and convince ourselves, "Oh, it is nothing. You are making a mountain out of a molehill. Stop worrying—you are such a scaredy-cat." And we listen to that inner critic and move on with our day.

It is not always easy to listen to these cryptic voices or to trust our gut. Our culture rarely trains us to as children, it is not a part of the curriculum in our education system, and our world does not put our clairvoyant gifts on the front page or at the top of the news hour. Most in our society would rather think about a problem in a linear way and solve it than spend time quietly listening to, trusting, and following their intuition. Some people even look down upon their sixth sense; they almost become uncomfortable and embarrassed when they have to talk about their intuition. They speak of it in whispers, hoping no one will judge them. Because of this I have so much compassion and understanding for people who hear their intuition but do not follow it.

Intuitive Guide: One Mother's Story

Most of my close friends and family knew I was writing a book on intuition. We would talk about it over dinner parties or on hikes, or when we'd meet to pick up our kids from activities or bump into each other at the grocery store. Usually they would kindly ask, "How is the book coming along?" I was flattered and grateful for their interest and would often talk about parts of the book where I was still looking for stories.

A dear friend passed on the name of a brave woman who was willing to tell me about a time she had felt a deep premonition about someone but did not listen to her intuition and afterward received one of the hardest and deepest teachings in her life.

I am so grateful this woman was courageous enough to share her story with me. I met her at a coffee shop. She appeared a bit shy and nervous, so we decided to take our drinks outside and sit on two rocks next to a busy street. We shook hands, and I tried to assure her that I would not write anything that she was uncomfortable with, or pester her about anything she didn't feel good telling me. Feeling her uneasiness, I was reminded of what an honor it is to bear witness to all of my intuitive guides' stories.

A Powerful Positive Meeting

Twice in her life, she had a super powerful experience meeting someone for the first time. "The first time it was an essentially positive, super epic, and intense moment. I turned around, saw this man, and pow, it hit me like a lightning bolt of recognition, like I had known him in a past life. That person became very important in my life in a lot of ways." He was a customer at the bar where she worked. They formed a friendship, and it was this friendship that carried her through her massive grief from losing her first child. Unexpectedly, he was there for her to support her during this awful time of loss and sadness. After developing this deep connection, one she felt would be in her life forever, he one day just up and disappeared. He did not return until ten years later, the exact time she needed him during another life struggle, when she was questioning her marriage. He helped her through this transition and then disappeared again.

A Powerful Negative Meeting

The second time an intuitive occurrence happened, it was not full of light; it was an experience of deep darkness.

In the fall of 2014, she was dropping off her eight-year-old daughter at an after-school program and saw a man nearby in a crowded room of parents, kids, and instructors. She instantly had another one of those monumental "pow" flashes. But this time her intuition was very negative. "It was a lightning bolt of bad, bad, bad," she said. "I turned around and saw him, and my whole body filled with fear."

I witnessed her whole body begin to go back to that moment, and I watched as the somatic reaction of trauma and fear washed over her. Her body froze up, and she began to quiver a bit. We stopped; I asked her if she needed a break and let her know we didn't have to move forward.

Her reaction reminds me how trauma can stay stored in the body. It may not affect your each and every moment, but it has a way, like plaque on your teeth, of sticking to your organs and inner being. Traumatic experiences can very often take over your life and influence all your daily decisions. They may force you to be scared anytime someone watches your children, or influence what career you chose. You may check your doors numerous times before going to sleep or look several times over your shoulder while walking down a street. As a clinician, I am very sensitive to this issue, and I knew I had to be careful and patient and have a soft touch to not retraumatize this woman.

"These bad feelings came eight months before the event," she continued, "but it was crazy in so many ways that I had such a powerful reaction to his presence, and I had never laid eyes on him before. It was literally a lightning bolt of negative, scary, bad, and fear. It was a feeling of dark energy, like a dark, sick entity. It is hard to explain, but it was so present."

Intuition Ignored

"I took these dark feelings and packaged them up and threw them away," she went on. "It was so negative, bad, and hard to explain. In general it is hard to trust your intuition on things that are positive, so it is really hard to trust your intuition when it is super negative and hard to explain. Especially if it is about a person you don't know at all, so you just put it away."

We have all been in this situation, where we have a hard time listening to our intuition. Even though her sixth sense was so powerful, she, like most of us would, found a way to justify not listening. "At the time, my children were happy at this activity, and this person did not have any contact with my children. So my feelings with him were irrelevant. There didn't seem to be any reason to respond to how I'd felt. He was extraneous to my life, so I ignored my reaction to him. It wasn't even fully formed as a cognitive thought of 'This is a bad man'—it was an intense but amorphous and subconscious negative feeling. It was easy to move away from because it was so powerfully yucky. I just felt the 'pow,' put it away, and kept moving through my day."

Intuition Acknowledged

Eight months after she felt these spine-chilling intuitive feelings, she picked up her daughter from an overnight trip. The moment her daughter got in the car, she was upset and told her mom it was because she did not get to sleep next to her best friend. Her mom asked her why this happened, and she said, "Because this man wanted to cuddle with me."

Alarm bells went off right away. "Immediately I was like, 'Holy shit,'" she told me. "I was totally freaking out, shaking, wanting to throw up. I had no idea this man would be there overnight, let alone that he would be alone with my children. And so I asked her some questions, not wanting to freak her out. Unfortunately, she could tell I was upset, so she got upset as well."

They drove home, and within an hour this brave soul of a mother called the police. She and her daughter were the first to report that this man had "cuddled" with her daughter—had actually sexually abused her. They were not the only ones that came forward. Many other victims soon spoke up, and it was revealed that he had been abusing girls for years.

The way it played out, her daughter didn't really know what was wrong because luckily she was not severely harmed. He touched her, but for some reason he was more focused on another child. "It is still so fucked up," the woman said, "but it could have been a lot worse."

She was adamant about the fact that despite the awful experience, they received amazing support from the legal and mental-health systems. The cops showed up within an hour and handled the case with love and care, and their town has a counseling center for the children and families in sexual-abuse cases. The courts were sensitive and handled her family with so much care. The judge, district attorneys, and victim-assistance people were amazing. The community of victims' families became a tight little group of hugging moms in the courtroom. She came to think of some of these professionals and other parents as friends.

Her daughter went through a tsunami of different emotions, one being guilt because she felt she had caused all this sudden ruckus. Guilt is one of the main reasons individuals don't come forward as children, sometimes waiting until much later in life to tell anyone. I heard a story once about two women who went to their grandfather's funeral. After they buried his body, they went straight to the police station and filed a sexual-abuse case against him for the times he violated them as children. One of their pieces of healing came from having the police and legal system hear their story. Even though he was dead, they were still alive to be heard.

Fortunately, by testifying and being heard right away, my intuitive guide and her daughter didn't have to suffer a lifetime before healing began. The verdict and outcome helped validate their feelings by confirming that his actions were wrong. "I hated seeing him in court, but everyone else was so amazing," she told me. "What if he was still doing this? He was put away for thirty years."

Awful situations such as these require immense courage. Yet sadly, children and adults are not always believed in sexual-abuse cases. People want to turn away from this darkness, because it is too hard and scary. They do not want to believe that someone they love was abused or was the abuser and are terrified it will tear apart their family, relationships, and lives.

But usually they all know the truth, and it is so damaging to the body and spirit when someone has the strength to come forward and tell their awful story but is not believed. The most monumental healing occurs when the adults believe a child's story and take action to right this awful wrong. This is what my intuitive guide's family felt, especially her daughter. They were heard and held with love, and justice was served.

At the time this mother had her dark intuitive feeling, she was overwhelmed with a lot going on in her life. "As much as I tucked it away, the lesson was still there. I have always been a pretty intuitive person, but it was so easy to second-guess myself, easy to disregard things and put them away, especially because the dark feelings were so inexplicable. So that is what I did, but after the fact, it was like I wanted to say, 'Listen to yourself next time. There is a reason why you felt this way. Believe in yourself and your body and soul's reaction to people and places.' Even though I buried that experience, it came back to me."

Intuitive Advice

The voices you hear and feelings you experience are valid and ever present. You can try to act like they are nonexistent and deny them, but they may still haunt you. But when you inquire further, ask for guidance, and stay open, you may find some answers.

"If you feel weirdness about someone," the mother continued, "do something about it! Don't just tuck it away because you do not know what you are feeling. You may be questioning, 'Is this my energy I am picking up on, or somebody else's energy? Is it past-life stuff?' Who knows what it is, but it does not matter; it is something, and you need to believe."

As she was speaking, an immense amount of strength, a power, was streaming through her body, and truth was coming through her words. It was as if she were channeling the archetype of the mother-warrior, who had to sacrifice something for the greater good of all. My intuitive guide's voice is forcing us all to wake up to the way we look at life, to start asking questions, to think differently, and most importantly to listen to our damn intuition when we feel something is real. Her words were validating the whole premise of this book, which is that we need to put our internal voices at the forefront of our lives, not only for the safety of our children, but also for all human life.

She looked over at me. "I have never told anyone this piece of this story. Unconsciously I didn't want to tell this story; I was not ready to step into that role. And then I came to a place of knowing that it isn't about me anymore. This is about other mothers walking into dance studios or with babysitters and saying, 'Shit, I feel something, and I have to listen to it. Who cares if I'm wrong? Consider, what do I have to lose by listening to myself, and what do I have to lose by not?'"

Feeling her strength, I thought this might be a good time for me to ask her a hard question. A question that none of us wants to think about during traumatic times, but one that is beneficial for the greater good. "If you could go back in time," I asked, "would you have done anything different?"

"I don't know," she said. "That is hard, because I would never choose to put my kid through that, but on the other hand, in general I feel like everything that happens is the way it is. As hard and awful as it was, I believe there is a deeper reason why my daughter was the one to report and I was the one to call the cops. People come into each other's lives to learn things from each other. We are here to bounce off each other and have experiences that form us." She went on to tell me that she feels like she and her daughter were here to be his teacher. "To be the truth—to say, no, you cannot do that, and we will speak up. He was a very sick man, and they want to believe he had conflict about his actions. And that they and the other victims and families were the ones to say, 'That behavior is wrong. It hurts people. You must stop it or be stopped by outside forces.'"

She later shared an insightful and wise perspective: "I said that I hated seeing the perpetrator in court, but that isn't exactly clear as to what I meant. It's not that I hated him—it's that it was deeply uncomfortable to be in his presence. I had the same unsettled feeling I had the first time I'd seen him—that he was sick. Not sick like twisted and perverted, though he was maybe that, too—but sick as in unwell, deeply not healthy in soul. He looked so lost and scared in court, and part of what made me uncomfortable was witnessing his discomfort. There were others in the courtroom who were very vengeful and righteous toward him, but I didn't feel that way. I did not feel sorry for him, exactly, but I did feel his humanity. As someone who feels others' emotions very strongly, it was tough for me to feel his discomfort and also my own simultaneously, to realize that none of us expected or wanted to be where we were, that at our core we are all just humans bouncing around in a complicated world and doing the best we can. The best he could do was pretty lousy, but I felt some compassion for him as a scared and shamed victim of bad decision making, which we all have been at some point."

I took a deep breath. I was amazed by her incredibly deep compassion and felt the intuitive nature of forgiveness on some level.

As if I were not there, this brave mother asked herself again, "Would I want to have this happen again? Never. But I look at my child now and don't know if she would be the same child. She is rock solid, and she used to not be rock solid. She was my anxious kid, and all of a sudden she is strong. Something gave her strength and resiliency. She is a force to be reckoned with, saying, 'Don't fuck with me.' This she knows is true.

"There is no doubt in my mind that my daughter now knows exactly what is appropriate with her body and what is not. The older she gets, the more vulnerable she is, in some ways, as a young woman, but I know she has that one down. And from this awful experience, she learned an incredibly valuable lesson. She knows that if anything ever happens to her again, she can tell someone and it is okay because they will believe her."

I had chills because what this mom was saying was that some of our best teachings come from our hardest moments. As parents we feel like we have superpowers, or the kryptonite to throw at others to protect our children from everything. But we actually have very little power, and the problem is that we don't want to admit we have very little power. We put so much pressure on ourselves to be these superheroes and are constantly feeling ashamed or like we are failing, all for an unattainable goal. It is not our job to protect our children from everything. If we wrap them in Bubble Wrap, we are inhibiting them from learning their greatest teachings around resiliency, bravery, self-knowing, and self-worth.

Through this challenging experience this mother learned about not only her child's resiliency, but also what was real and not real in the whole situation. She realized that both the safety of the after-school center and this man's portrayal of himself as an honest caretaker were not real. The one thing that was real was her initial intuition. The darkness she felt, her gut instinct, and the voices that told her this was not a safe man were real. Because of her "real" dark intuitive feelings, she felt validated in later reporting the abuse to the police.

We were sitting quietly for a moment when she calmly said she needed to go grab her kids for an appointment. As she stood up, she turned to me and said, "Everyone feels it before [it happens], and sometimes they have control of it and sometimes they don't. Take the shame away from saying, 'I should have done something different,' and throw it away, because that is not always what it is about."

We hugged each other for quite some time. I hoped our embrace would energetically let her know how grateful I was for her courage to come forth and share her heart-wrenching story so all of us could learn how important it is to listen to our intuition. There is a power in telling your stories; we call it "narrative healing" in the therapy world. I watched her walk down the cobbled street with a different stride than she had when she arrived. And then I heard a loud voice inside me say, "Love can save you." Her love was the driving force that helped heal her daughter and herself, and it's love that helps heal all other abuse survivors, too.

CHAPTER 11

Here's something to think about: How come you never see a headline like "Psychic Wins Lottery"?

—Jay Leno

Imagine the last time you did something outside your comfort zone. You may have attended a party where you did not know many people, or participated in a cause that pushed your opinions or childhood dogmas in a new direction. Whatever the situation, you allowed yourself to stop being complacent, step out of your box, and enter the unknown. When you enter this unknown and open yourself up to hear, feel, and experience what resonates with you and your body, your intuition comes alive and you learn so much more about yourself. You may have never thought you loved sushi, shamanism, or skiing until you tried these things. You may have never met the love of your life if you did not open yourself up to participating in a dating app. You may have never gotten over your fear of heights until you tried bungee jumping.

Part of this intuitive journey is about looking at your fears and preconceived notions and challenging yourself by asking these questions:

"Could there be more to life?" "Where am I holding myself back to new experiences, people, or places out of fear or shame?" "Why am I not fulfilling my greatest potential?"

By opening up your mind, heart, and soul to new experiences, you are combating the dogmas that don't serve you anymore. I learned this by interviewing a medium, a person who talks to spirits in the afterlife. I opened myself up not only to a reading, but also to the truth that mediums have a deep connection to their intuition.

Meeting a Medium

I am a seeker. My deepest teachings and inspirations come from my spiritual journeys, because every time I answer the call to a pilgrimage I become more connected to my higher self and grow into a better person, a more present wife and mother, and a more available guide for my clients. Some of my most important spiritual teachings come by learning the stories of others' spiritual journeys and then taking them myself. My desire to learn others' stories is how I found myself in a session with a medium.

One afternoon I was telling a friend about my book on intuition. "Oh, you have to talk to Austyn Wells," she said, excited. "She is a medium and a dear friend of my sister who lives in Los Angeles." She told me about how once, while she was visiting her sister, Austyn came over to do an intuitive reading for her and a group of her friends, and my friend gushed about how amazing she was. The seeker side of me knew immediately that I needed to speak with Austyn about intuition.

I emailed her and asked if she would be interested in being in my book. She responded quite quickly, so swift it made me wonder if she had already known that I was going to send her a note. She was incredibly open to being in the book. So that the reading would be as authentic as possible, we agreed it would be best if she did an intuitive reading with me first, before our interview. Even though I am a spiritual seeker, a part of me was skeptical about mediums, I asked her if it would be okay if we Skyped. Unconsciously, I wanted to see her face and reactions to ensure authenticity.

The day arrived for my intuitive reading, and I had butterflies in my stomach—what would she tell me? I was shocked that I felt nervous, as I have often dipped my toe into the metaphysical world. To calm my nerves I went up to my bedroom and got situated. I lit a candle, made a cup of tea, and said a prayer to help me stay open to whatever I was about to hear, despite my skepticism, the same skepticism I had as a child when I went to confession. I never had the screen between the priest and me. With all the courage I could muster, I would come around the corner to confess my sins to the priest face to face. "If I am going to confess my sins," I would tell myself, "I want to do it in person." Then I knew I could watch the priest tell God and I would be forgiven. As my medium session was going to be a somewhat confessional experience, I wanted to be face to face—via Skype—with Austyn as well.

The moment I saw Austyn's angelic face and warm smile I knew I was in good hands. I loved that she laughed within the first few minutes, and I did not have to see floating moons, twinkling stars, or purple sparkling fabric in the background. She chose to sit outside her home in Los Angeles with the hills surrounding her and the hummingbirds as her companions.

We connected with a smile and both shared how excited we were to go on this intuitive journey together. The session was supposed to last an hour and a half, but we spent two and a half hours together. Time moved so quickly, and it felt as if I were only with Austyn for a few moments.

To put this life-changing experience into words is quite difficult. She was able to tap into the spirit world and have the spirits share things about me that nobody else would have known—the names of my brothers, for instance, the fact that my father had died in October, and the fact that I was drawn to India and had spent time at an orphanage there, and it was where I felt my most content. Austyn nailed my perfectionism and spoke about how I hid it well, and not many people in my life would know this about me.

She talked about how at five one morning my mom walked out to see two hearts mysteriously carved in her snowy driveway, with no tracks or footprints around. Austyn said it was my dead father telling my mother he loved her.

As the session was ending and we were saying our goodbyes, I experienced a wave of gratitude. Austyn had reconnected me to myself. She did not tell me my future; she reminded me of who I was in the present and that I had a lot inside me that was creative, resilient, and intuitive.

My reading reminded me that the most authentic way of being is to be myself. To not get caught up in things that are not my soul's calling—the ego, jealousy, greed, or comparison. Austyn emphasized that I was strong and needed to remember to move forward instead of getting caught in useless energies.

I was incredibly excited to hear more from Austyn about her story, how intuition played a part in her life, and what her mediumship could teach us about intuition.

Intuitive Guide: Austyn Wells

Austyn Wells grew up in the mecca of the spiritual world, Northern California, right outside of San Francisco. Her journey into the intuitive world began when she was five. Her mom had wanted her to be in a fashion show, but Austyn was nervous and afraid she was going to trip or fall. The night before the fashion show, she woke up terrified. Other nights when this would happen she knew her mom was not the one to go to for help. "Not being able to go to my mom when I was scared was perfect," she told me, "because it taught me that prayer works." So instead of running to her mom's room, she prayed from the bottom of her soul to relieve some of her fears.

When she prayed, the walls in her bedroom suddenly began to morph, and her room filled with ghostlike figures. "One beautiful woman came to the side of my bed, and I was not one bit scared. She communicated with me, soul to soul. It was an invisible and quiet language. She knew I was scared and asked me if I needed her." Then her bedroom became two realities. One side of the room was filled with all the ghostly people, and the other side was the future runway show.

"I watched myself walking down the runway, nervous, but really having fun. Although I was still scared, I knew I would be okay." The angelic figure let Austyn experience the energy of the audience. She could feel how much they loved and supported her. "There was an immense amount of positive energy in the entire room."

Austyn breathed softly, remembering this moment. "It was not just me; it was the people and the spiritual presence surrounding me."

In a flash, as if in a science-fiction movie, Austyn was back in her bedroom with the angel letting her know she would be okay. Then they all disappeared.

"Since that experience I have always known I was going to be okay."

Another time young Austyn had an encounter with the other side, a dog was involved. Every day she walked to school she would stop to tell it hello. One morning, after giving the dog her daily hug, she heard it say, "Thank you for loving me. I will miss you." She turned around and thought, "I will miss you, too." Sadly, on the way home from school, Austyn found out the dog had been hit by a car and died that afternoon.

She did not have any similar experiences for some time. Austyn believes the spirit world realized she was too open and didn't want her to be afraid, because in the future she would need to help other people connect to the spirits.

"I had instincts and knew prayer worked, but it wasn't until I was eighteen years old that my intuitive ability popped open again.

Experiences starting happening at my boyfriend's house, and I knew I was guided by something bigger. Thank goodness his mother encouraged me to develop this skill. She became a great spiritual guide through this time."

From then on Austyn jumped in with two feet and started doing intuitive readings for private parties. She did over two thousand different events. Even though she felt invigorated, she didn't have anyone to turn to for advice about her gift. "I began to read anything I could get my hands on, because I would think, 'What the hell is going on with me?'" Then, a few years before her father died, the spirit world said, "We are going to use you differently now."

After Austyn had told me about her beginnings, I asked, "What does intuition mean to you?"

"The first part of intuition that is important to me is the first two letters, *i-n*. It is an inner listening. Listening to your soul. Your soul is inspired by many other souls that are connected to your evolution. In intuition there is the presence of your higher self or the aspect of the soul that will always be tethered to the divine. Intuition is a higher wisdom and comes as a very small, still voice."

"Being that it is a small voice," I asked, "how do you access your intuition?"

"I have to be in my intuition to work. My work is so gratifying because I am only in the moment that is presenting itself. In order to access my intuition, I have to be completely present and not distracted by my own cock-a-doodle-doo."

We laughed because we both understand this cock-a-doodle-do— the mind busy with regrets and worries. We also both know that one of the keys to tapping into one's intuition is being still and present to hear its wisdom.

"My intuition is like a musical instrument," Austyn said, "and the soul in the spirit world is the musician. As their melody plays, I will feel, sense, taste, hear, and know elements of how their story unfolded.

Sometimes there is harmony and other times dissonance. My work is best when I am simply the instrument and just allow the soul's symphony to play. . . . It's amazing how subtle the messages are. People expect communication from the spirit world to come crashing in like a one-man band, but it is incredible how quiet it is. The beauty of this work is sitting in that serenity of the spirit world. Intuition is deeply personal and nourishing. There is a reason why they don't come crashing in, so we can learn to listen."

Austyn paused, as if reconsidering. "Well, there are times when they come crashing in, when they need to get our attention," she clarified. "The spirit world cannot change our lives, as they cannot live for us. However, they can help support or try to wake us up. Their intention is always loving. But generally they are quiet in order to teach us to become more still within ourselves."

"How do you help people connect to their intuition?" I asked.

"By reminding people to feel more into their life than think into their life. The soul feels life, as it is inspired by passion. It senses life. That's how mediums work with their 'clair,' or clear senses—clairsentience, clairaudience, or clairvoyance—because it's all about having feelings in order to feel life."

Austyn's words remind me of our five senses, and the importance of incorporating our sixth sense, our intuition, into our daily lives. I often have clients who come in feeling quite anxious or unsettled. I will guide them to let go of their other senses by breathing, and relaxing into the present moment, and by doing so they connect to their intuition and have a strong knowing that everything will be okay. Their sixth sense has reassured them and given them hope.

Austyn shared her take on our other senses. "It's amazing to get someone to sit in a room and take a moment to listen to the sounds of the room. Focus on one sense, like how their body feels in a chair or what sounds they hear outside. Humans capture their lives so much with sight. It is the reason why we have issues, because we are buying into the illusion of what we see is the truth, but I believe what we feel is really the truth. . . . Because we are looking more outside ourselves perhaps than looking inside, bridging to our intuition is mandatory. It is the balancer for us to be able to take in life on the inside and allow ourselves [an] authentic soul response by checking in with ourselves."

I was reminded of the scientific community's skepticism around mediumship and intuition, so I asked, "What is your opinion about the research that says intuition or the spirit world is not real?"

"We need to question and doubt," Austyn said. "We must allow for all opinions and responses. Science and spirituality are great balancers. Science is being influenced by spirituality, and spirituality is yearning for the validation of science. . . . I love the brain. I think it is the sexiest part of us by far. Think about the integration of the brain and intuition as a piece of art. Picture a canvas; the analytical part of our brain would be the circumstances of life. It would be drawn out as the outline of a building, the definition of the space logically, but it is the intuition or creativity of the soul that comes in and adds the hues of color and makes your canvas completely different from everyone else's. We need both, or it will lack definition. If we have too much definition, we miss the beauty, and at the same time we need the definition to hold the space for beauty. The beauty and the definition have to dance together."

The metaphor of a piece of art to describe the integration between the brain and our intuition is spot-on. We need both the left and right sides of our brain for stability and wholeness.

"I won't defend my work, because I appreciate skeptics," she said. "We need people to doubt; they are the control group in our experiment. In order for any science experiment to work, you need the person who is biased and the person who is unbiased in order for something to be proven. There are people that this will not work for, and that's perfect, because I honestly believe their soul is not meant to follow this path. I have witnessed when people experience things outside of what is known to them. . . . They may become overwhelmed, or confused, or confounded. It is at this point their soul can lead them upon a new journey. It is at that point that people begin to listen to themselves differently. At first it may feel like a foreign language, but with time, it becomes a dear and trusted friend."

I witness this often with my clients. They will identify as an atheist or nonbeliever who feels that intuition, religion, or spirituality are things other people need. And then tragedy hits—a death, divorce, or disease—and they grasp for something outside themselves for support. At times they reach for spirituality or religion to find peace. Other times they still identify as atheist but discover more solidarity and uncover more depth in their life by opening their minds to different approaches.

As we continued to speak about connecting to one's soul, Austyn began to talk with excitement: "There are absolutely souls that come into this world who do not experience any spirituality at all, by choice. Before the soul comes in the body, there is cohesion and a oneness in the spirit world; there is not a sense of separation. Yet, once the soul distills into the body, it is contained, and there is an appearance from the outside that it is an individual separate from the whole. Part of the experiment of being on this planet is to see what happens when that sense of oneness is removed, [when individuals feel] they are on their own. Do they seek community? Do they seek God or not? Do they become obsessed with material possessions? Do they become overwhelmed with greed? Do they become obsessed with what the Bible calls 'the sins of man'? We need every sort of expression in order to learn. Sadly, we need people who do incredible harm, because then incredible gratitude and grace comes out of it. We learn by contrast. It's unfortunate we have to have complete opposites to learn, yet the contrast is truly perfection."

I was drawn in deeper at this point because as a Jungian analyst I am an advocate for the dark and the light. "There is no coming to consciousness without pain," Carl Jung said. "People will do anything, no matter how absurd, in order to avoid facing their own soul." The darkness is essential for healing.

"One of the principles in the spirit world is: retribution is open to all souls," Austyn continued. "There is a desire to describe something as dark or light or something as good or bad. I know it is how our brain solves things. By categorizing things or judging things, we miss so much beauty. There is so much beauty in darkness. Our darkness is equally delicious and profound."

I could not agree more. Embracing your darkness—your jealousy and rage, your envy and loss—is essential for healing.

"I find no matter how dark a person's perception is, once they explore it like a dimension, it will appear dark, but it will always have a shaft of light, an illuminating presence somewhere. I have never had a client go to the dark and not find light."

Austyn went on to clarify that as a medium she does not heal someone. She offers the potential for someone to step into themselves more deeply in order to self-heal. "We are just channels," she said.

As we came to the end of our time together, I wanted to know if Austyn, as a "scientist" to the spirit world, had any last thoughts to share.

"Intuition has to happen when you are really listening to yourself. It comes from within. We have to have the courage and patience to nurture that relationship, because it's the foundation on which our soul can express itself. We are here to dip deeply into our soul and let that magic of the individual grace this world. . . . We are all meant to get caught up in the chaos, but the intuition and voice of soul is the sanity, and it's the eye of the storm. You cannot change the storm, but you can alter your involvement in it by relaxing into yourself.

It doesn't come from anything other than making time, place, and space for the soul."

An intuitive junkie, I could not help but get one more hit. I asked Austyn one more question: "What have been some of your deepest teachings?"

"That there is a universe inside just waiting. There is already a part of your soul that has always existed in that place and space. An aspect of us is always tethered to that infinite intelligence or divine essence. It is that tether that can take you deep into incredible, insatiable beauty."

My heart soared because Austyn was speaking to what I innately know, that the human race is coming into a time where we must seriously consider making our intuition take precedence. If we can embrace this tethering, we will find immense life satisfaction.

"My hope is if we have the ability to communicate to other greater intelligences," she continued, "why are we not using it for world peace? Why are we not using it as a global think tank to get a group of people together with the integrity for the highest good? They can channel the wisdom of those who have lived before or those that guide this world. Instead of arguing about who is right or wrong, we could just listen. We should talk less and listen more."

She was quiet and contemplative for a moment. I believe she was connecting to other worlds.

"We are listening more to the outside of ourselves than within, and there is so much help within. It takes time to develop intuition because our trust has gotten shaken, and there is a reason for it. I have never been deceived by the spirit world. There is a constant companion there. We are inconsistent in our behavior, but that inner wisdom can help us learn from what happens, so we can be the best version of ourselves. I am aware of what the pure potential of us is when we are connected to that divine source. I'm equally aware that the potential is in every single human being I encounter and they just have forgotten it or they are not supposed to remember it, and that helps me with my compassion."

In that moment I felt we both knew she was speaking pure truth, nothing more and nothing less.

She took a deep breath. "It's a magical journey to fall in love with your soul, and from that place comes the awareness that we are surrounded by unconditional love. When we evolve to the best versions of ourselves, our compassion and gratitude expand and our desire to be of service shifts to the forefront. From this place, we can change the world. It is time for all of us to make this kind of soul commitment, because our contrast is becoming extraordinary. Perhaps with the outside volume so loud, we will seek the quiet inside and bathe in the garden of our soul."

Enough said.

CHAPTER 12

INTEGRATION OF THE HEAD AND THE HEART FOR DEEPER INTUITION

He who works with his hands is a laborer. He who works with his hands and his head is a craftsman. He who works with his hands and his head and his heart is an artist.

—Often attributed to Saint
Francis of Assisi

Some things in life need a partner to be complete. Batman would not be as successful without Robin by his side. A peanut butter sandwich would not taste as delicious if it did not have jelly. And who would have watched *Friends* without the romantic back-and-forth of Ross and Rachel?

Intuition relies on a partnership, too, a partnership between one's head and one's heart. You can also call it a partnership between science and spirituality, or between the analytical mind and the mystical spirit; it does not matter. What is important is the integration of these two worlds.

The Dalai Lama speaks of this integration: "This is my simple religion. There is no need for temples; no need for complicated philosophy.

Our own brain, our own heart is our temple; the philosophy is kindness." The Sufi religion touches on this marriage of mind and soul, too, in a saying about using your head to be in service to your heart and about how one can lead the other, but they are never without each other.

Just as the Sufis say, there are times when you need to use the head, which is more analytical and logical, to solve a problem, and times when you need to listen to your heart, which is more spiritual, to follow a voice that is right for you. And then there are times you need to access both your head and heart to be more whole. The two are not so disconnected to begin with; they are more alike than different. And by broadening your scope and combining these two parts of yourself, you open up all your physical and energetic channels to allow intuition to live in your entire body, you calibrate your internal compass, and you create an intimacy with your internal wisdom (your psyche, dreams, and soul) while expanding your external world (your relationships, passions, and everyday decisions).

I learned about knitting together the two worlds of the head and the heart when I was twenty-nine and teaching at an all-girls private school in San Francisco, California. I adored the girls and their families, and I felt so fortunate to be in a career where I felt alive, creative, and in the field of education. I had no intention of changing careers, nor did I have a wandering eye for other opportunities. I was very content and secure with being a teacher.

One morning, as I was scurrying around getting ready for the day, the head of the lower school walked into my classroom. "Molly, I think you should look into being a school counselor," she said. "You are really good with the kids that are struggling." My jaw dropped. "I would never want to be a counselor," I thought, "sitting all day listening to people's problems." In that moment my mind was closed, and counseling was the last thing I thought I would ever do for a job.

Well, fast-forward a year later. Out at a loud bar in the Marina District of San Francisco, having drinks with a group of friends, I overheard an acquaintance talking about a master's program he was attending in Santa Barbara. He mentioned it was around Jungian psychology, the soul, neurobiology, teaching, and dream work. As my ears were ringing, my intuition was instantly intrigued. Somehow my mind opened up, and I was fascinated by the way a graduate school could create a master's counseling program that blended psychology and science of the mind with the mystical. Isn't it surprising, I thought, how this counseling opportunity is arising again but that now my intuition is saying yes and the idea is resonating with me? It was a timing thing; it was as if a seed had been planted a year prior and the universe only now had it grow. Sitting restless on a cold stool, my soul was ignited by the possibility of attending a master's program that would have classes around the concepts of therapeutic process and the callings of the soul.

Six months later I attended my first class at Pacifica Graduate Institute. Graduate school prepared me to be an excellent therapist. Even better, it reinforced the importance of creating a multifaceted, integrated life, of living in both sides of the brain, and of opening up my heart and soul to many ways of looking at the world, healing, and education. It was in this oneness that I strengthened my therapeutic intuition and my sense of self.

While researching this area of the book, I came across so many articles with titles like "Is It Better to Use Your Head or Heart When Faced with Decisions?" or "Head vs. Heart: Which Is Smarter?" These titles conjure an image of two body parts in a boxing ring, ready to have the match of the century. I believe this is a false image; it is not beneficial to pit head and heart against each other.

I understand why these articles are written, however. The marriage of these two parts often makes people uncomfortable. Like politics and religion, these concepts don't always mix at dinner parties. Watch what happens when people talk about a topic analytically and are then asked about how that makes them feel. Or when someone is sharing a story about an emotional subject and then you ask him or her a logistical question. They stop talking and appear almost confused. Switching from the head to the heart and vice versa can be challenging, because it pushes against your boundaries, values, and ideas, but you must if you want experience a oneness of being.

Left Brain

To create this wholeness of self, and to have a more rooted relationship with our intuition, let's learn more about ourselves, starting with the brain. Even though intuition resides in the right hemisphere of the brain, it is important to integrate both the left and right sides for emotional balance and deeper intuition. How do you know if you are living too much in your left brain? Ask yourself these questions:

- Am I feeling overly controlling?
- Am I unable to let things go, fixating or obsessing over a place, person, or situation?
- Am I focusing too much on my external world of logistics, and not enough on my internal world of emotions?

If you live too much in the left side of your brain, the linear and logical side, you will cut yourself off from your feelings, and once you do experience an emotion—fear, sadness, or even joy—you may feel frozen, lost, or uncomfortable. You may even decide to numb yourself with food, alcohol, or shopping to inhibit feeling out of control.

To resume balance in the brain, try to connect to your right side. Start by noticing what is going on in your body by asking yourself some questions: "Is my heart racing?" "How does my stomach feel?" "What is my heart telling me to do?" "What emotions are arising when I am in this situation?" "What do I do when I feel an emotion?"

A story close to my heart exemplifies balancing the left and right sides of the brain. My husband is a scientist who often lives in his logical mind. After he applied to graduate school for biochemistry and began receiving his acceptance letters, he was trying to decide which program he wished to attend. The questions that kept arising for him were "Where would I want to live?" and "Which school is the most prestigious?" and "Whose lab would I wish to be a part of?"

After struggling with these questions for weeks, he went down to his local bar, put all the universities' names on a dartboard, and threw darts at them. When the dart landed on one of the schools, he would ask himself, "How do I feel imagining going to this school? Am I excited, disappointed, elated, or sad?" Little did he know that the gift he was giving himself was balancing out the logical and emotional sides of his brain. By playing this emotional dart game, he eventually had a clear answer. The moment the dart landed on the University of California–San Francisco, he felt his intuition for the first time and knew clearly where to go.

Right Brain

An imbalance also occurs when you live too heavily on the right hemisphere of the brain, the creative and insightful part. You will discover you have excessive emotions, or, as we therapists call it, a "flooding" of emotions, with no balance or grounding. In order to calm down, you need to be more logical and linear to bring the two hemispheres together. If you think you might be living too much in your right brain, ask yourself these questions:

- Am I overly emotional over certain topics?
- Am I having a hard time separating from my feelings?
- Am I unable to function in my day-to-day responsibilities because of my emotions?

How do you rebalance and create harmony between your right and left hemispheres? When you feel out of control with your emotions, get out of your emotional state and into your logistical life. Begin by doing a task—clean your closet, put the dishes in the dishwasher, jump up and down, or make a pros-and-cons list about your challenging situation. Then ask yourself, "What should I do next?" or "What steps can I take to alleviate this painful situation?" or "Where do I go from here?"

Once a client of mine was too heavy in the right brain and overwhelmed with emotions. She had discovered her husband was having an affair, and felt incredibly hurt, angry, and betrayed. Emotions were flying all over the room, and she could not see beyond any of them. I knew she was flooding with emotion in her right brain, so I attempted to have her connect with her left brain. I had her talk about the details of when and how she discovered the affair. I kindly asked her where in her body she was the most triggered and whether she remembered anything anyone had said to her that brought her some ease or allowed her to see outside her emotions. By bringing her into the body, and the here and now, I was able to help her ground herself, calm down, and think more logically about her situation. With greater balance, she realized that no matter what happened she would survive; it would be hard as hell, but she would live. I don't mean to simplify a very challenging situation, but when you are drowning in your emotions, being more logical can help you feel more secure and stable in order to handle whatever situation may arise. When both sides of the brain are integrated, emotional stability is created, allowing intuition to be more readily available.

Heart and Soul

Enhancing your relationship with your soul leads to even greater balance, and a deeper connection to your intuition. To describe the soul in a couple of paragraphs is like attempting to describe God, the unconscious, or nature—it is practically impossible. But what I hope to accomplish is to help you learn how to trust it.

Think of the soul as a silo, a gigantic one: 90 feet in diameter and 275 feet high. This silo is filled with water, and only one drop is the body, the rest the soul. The soul is massive compared to the body. In fact, no, the soul is endless. It expands way beyond the container of the body, lives deep in the belly of your psyche, and drives many of your decisions and passions. Your memories of the past, experiences of the present, and ability to trust the unknown future are all contained within the soul's vastness, as are your passions, dreams, and relationships. Like the universe, the soul is never-ending, forever expanding yet the center of your being. Speaking of space, if you love *Star Trek*, the soul is your Starfleet headquarters. It is where you go back to refuel and remind yourself who you are and what your mission is.

The soul is the mecca of your spiritual experiences. When you find a way to have a relationship with the depths of your soul, you learn to hear the difference between your intuition and your wounds, your truth and your lies. Dean Koontz says it beautifully: "Intuition is seeing with the soul." The soul and intuition are as connected as our bones are to our tendons, or our hearts are to our children. There is not one without the other. Intuition is your soul's guidance system.

It takes faith to trust the soul. It is not like trusting that a chair will hold your body. The soul is not external; we cannot grab it with our two hands and hold it for validity of truth. The soul is not solid; it is a symbol or feeling that is forever evolving.

The soul and intuition are so intertwined because they both live in the same family of the unseen, the internal, and the mysterious. The Sufi poet Rumi knew this: "Oh soul, you worry too much. You have seen your own strength. You have seen your own beauty. You have seen your golden wings. Of anything less, why do you worry? You are in truth the soul, of the soul, of the soul." Living in the soul comes down to trust, trusting that what you hear, feel, and experience will guide you to live your most fulfilling life.

Putting It All into Practice

Now that you know the gift of balancing the left and right sides of your brain, and of having a relationship with your soul or heart, what do these gifts look like on a practical level?

They look like a weekly meditation class, for instance, followed by listening to NPR on your way home. Or attending classes on the chakras and classes on IT systems. Or going to your Sunday service of choice and reading a book on atheism. Or playing in both the spiritual and rational worlds, being open to the mysteries of life while embracing the concepts you already know to be true. Or not always taking things at face value and continuing to research topics that intrigue you and force you to face your fears. This balanced dance of living in both the right and left brains will clear a pathway for your intuition to thrive.

Think of the brain and the heart as a series of doors. The more doors you keep closed—based on fear, lack of control, or negative internal scripts such as "Oh, I am not comfortable with that idea" or "My religion or culture does not believe in that concept"—the greater your risk of trapping yourself in a smaller room of life. But the more doors you open, the more you can experience life. Open the doors! Yearn to be an explorer of the inner workings of your mind, and a voyager of your mysterious heart. Stay curious and ask the big questions in life, and do not shy away from bearing witness to your expansions and contractions. Don't be afraid. Even if it makes you feel uncomfortable or does not totally resonate with you, try it, let your body feel a different experience, and watch how your connection deepens to your intuition, yourself, and the universal force in us all.

Chew on these ideas. Think about your life and how you can open yourself up to live in both your head and your heart. Stop for a moment, close your eyes, and put yourself in a situation where you only came from your head or from your heart. Notice how you feel. Now try to blend both your head and your heart. You may feel uncomfortable and awkward, or you may feel more integrated and whole, with more access to ideas on how to solve a problem or heal a wound. Now go even deeper, and ask yourself: "Where am I getting stuck in life?" "Why do I close myself off to different ideas and beliefs?" "Am I uncomfortable with living in both my head and my heart? And if so, why?"

Now open your eyes and notice your body, biases, and beliefs. Do you feel more complete, as if you have more access to a broader world of both analytical and mystical skills? In this peaceful and open-minded place, consider where in your life you integrate every part of yourself. Where do you hold yourself back out of fear and insecurity? When you follow not only your mind but also your heart, do you feel more alive? Where is your Batman and Robin?

I have had to ask myself these questions many times—like when I opened my mind to switching careers. I am so grateful that the head of my lower school followed her intuition to come into my classroom and inspire me to go in a different educational direction. At the Pacifica Graduate Institute I realized that my mind and heart could be integrated and then open, stretch, and grow in order to create a deeper sense of peace and intuition. At twenty-seven I learned that when I am judgmental and put things into boxes out of fear, dogma, or preconceived beliefs, I am lonelier and angrier and feel a sense of dismemberment from life. Luckily, I also learned that by integrating my head and my heart, my brain and my soul, I am much more available to life—to have fun, to meet new people, to learn new and amazing ideas. I stretch, am more expansive and alive. I learned that my peanut butter sandwich is so much better with jelly, and that my heart is so much happier when I can also use my head.

CHAPTER 13

MY JOURNEY: BARCELONA

Changing is not changing the things outside of us. First of all we need the right view that transcends all notions including of being and non-being, creator and creature, mind and spirit. That kind of insight is crucial for transformation and healing.

—*Thich Nhat Hanh*

In the winter of 2016 I accepted a job as a high school counselor at the American School of Barcelona, in Spain. I had lived in Barcelona from 1997 to 1999, working as a second-grade teacher at another American school. Because of this life-changing experience, my husband and I had talked for years about moving our family to another country and then finally decided to.

During the chaos, I applied for our visas, told our friends and family we were moving, started packing, tried to rent our house, and put check marks on our incredibly long to-do list. I continued to unconsciously believe that I had control over my life, and I convinced myself that my intuition was speaking to me loud and clear. I thought my plan was rock solid, especially since I am someone that trusts her sixth sense as her compass for the truth.

Then life slapped me right across the face one balmy afternoon as I returned home after picking up some visa paperwork from the post office. I pulled into my driveway hot and annoyed. My ten-year-old son was telling me soccer statistics while my eight-year-old daughter was belting out Taylor Swift lyrics at the top of her lungs. My cell phone began ringing its as-Buddhist-as-you-can-get ringtone. It was my brother. The kids opened the car doors and ran inside to grab their sugary snacks and iPads, and I swiftly fumbled to push the accept button, knowing my brother had spent the day with my youthful, healthy mom at the doctor's office.

"Hi, Michael," I gasped.

There was a long pause on the other end. "Where are you, Molly?" he said.

"I am in my garage."

"Am I on speakerphone? Are the kids in the car?"

"No, I am alone. Michael, you are starting to scare me. What's going on?"

My six-foot collegiate-football-star brother started breathing heavily with a stifled voice, and I thought he might cry.

"Molly, Mom has cancer," he said.

With those four words, I wanted to throw up in my white Toyota Highlander.

My brother continued using his left brain and gave me the details. "There is an exterior tumor on her ampullary bile duct. She is a candidate for the Whipple surgery, and then she will have to have chemotherapy."

In disbelief, I thought to myself, "What the hell? She can't have cancer. She is healthy as a horse. Dad died five years ago—I don't want to lose another parent. I don't want to lose my mother, whom I love dearly. Holy shit! My family is supposed to move to Spain in five months."

My brother responded, but his words began to sound like a mumbling adult character from *Peanuts*. I was in a state of anger, fear, despair, and immense grief. I found myself sinking into a swamp of victimhood. "Oh no, not again."

And I had to breathe. I had to breathe to get off the phone and into my house, make the family dinner, and try to keep it somewhat together so that my kids did not see me totally lose my shit. As I moved through my evening in a thick fog, I began to feel the bodily sensations of grief. I felt numb, my temper was short, and a dread as heavy as a brick house landed on my chest.

A week later I was putting my kids to bed and having a moment of silence when I suddenly had a sense of light, levity, and release. I could not grasp what this was all about. "Molly, you just found out your mom has cancer," I heard a voice inside me say. "What the hell are you happy about?"

Then came to me these words: "You have a way out. You may not have to move to Spain."

The week I learned of my mom's cancer diagnosis, I also received my "get out of jail free" card. I could tell my community and myself that the reason I was not moving to Spain was that my mom had cancer, versus telling the embarrassing truth that the move was not right for our family at the time, and that I was secretly living the exotic dream of "Our family is moving to Spain; aren't we so adventurous and brave?" The younger, egoic part of myself that is a pleaser wanted to use this cancerous excuse.

Because what no one knew in my life—not my husband, family, or friends—was that from the moment I started interviewing for the job in Barcelona, which was a "job of a lifetime," I felt an uneasy pull in my gut that it was not the right decision. Not wanting to look at my confusion, I had ignored this feeling at all costs and stuffed it in a locked box never to open it again.

But the voices and uneasy feelings had not gone away. I tried to coerce them into disappearing by telling myself, "If you get the job, you are supposed to go," but even after receiving the job my chest would

131

feel tight. "Oh, you are just nervous," I would tell myself, trying to shrug it off. I didn't want to listen. I didn't want to look deeper. It was too scary. So I kept moving forward, believing I had control over this situation, control over my body, and control over my life. "Molly, what is wrong with you?" I continued to ask myself. "This is your choice and is an incredible opportunity. Pull it together." But I couldn't pull it together, because unconsciously I think I knew all along that it was not the right decision.

My mom's heartbreaking diagnosis, however, forced me to finally get honest with myself. I realized it was not my intuition pointing me toward Barcelona and the excitement of a new life there; it was my ego. I had tried to justify and rationalize otherwise, but it was true. Even though ego and intuition can be confusing and look the same way, they are innately different. The ego is not always clear, or peaceful. It can be alluring and delusional, and it has a way of convincing you to do, be, or say something that does not feel right. When you are in this state, you will find yourself overidentifying with an idea, which in my case was "Oh, isn't my family so amazing and unique because we are moving to Spain?" The whole time we were preparing to go, it felt dramatic, as if things were working against us, which fed my ego.

I was letting my ego make my decision partly because I wanted to run away from my loneliness, anxiety, and boredom. I wanted to pull the ripcord on my life and live a grass-is-always-greener lifestyle in Spain. I needed to revive my marriage from its routine pressures and logistics: "Who's making breakfast?" and "Did you pay the bills?" and "What time are we supposed to pick up Tommy from soccer?" And I needed an escape from the weight of all those stories I heard in my clinical practice, an escape to save my kids from the wonderful but also intense, and intensely homogenous, world that I tended to buy in to. I was aware of how fortunate I was, but there's always a shadow side to life—the unknown or dark side of one's personality, family, institution, or organization that we don't always want to address—and the environment I lived in was full of high expectations, ego, perfectionism, and an inherent pressure to fit in, to keep up with the Joneses. It was hard to be vulnerable, and I felt like I was living in a box.

Ultimately, however, part of me had to die. I had to surrender and let go of my egoic dream of moving to Barcelona, let it burn away, turn into ashes to be spiritually reborn. This death forced me to dive deep into my heart, face fears, and tell the truth in order to remember to let go of the life I thought I would have, to embrace the life that was in front of my eyes. I needed to realize I was separate from my ego, and it was my heart that gave meaning to my life. Even though my ego wanted to be sipping wine in this beautiful European city, my intuition knew that in order to find my soul I needed to spend my time in the States, taking care of my kids, going home to see my mom—who is now healthy and strong—and writing a book about intuition in a community-college library. I had to face the friends and family that were saying, "There are airplanes" or "You will not have this opportunity again" and listen to the voice—not of the ego, but of intuition—that was saying, "This is not the right time to move to Spain, and you will not know all the reasons why, but you must listen and trust."

My mom's diagnosis came with a ton of sadness, but it was also my ticket to freedom, my ticket to be honest, to lose control, to be humbled, raw, and real with my intuition. Because, you see, intuition has no agenda. This sixth sense that we all have—I mean each and every one of us—resides in the heart and only wants us to live authentically. It may not always look pretty or feel good, but it always has our best interests in mind.

Before this experience, I thought I was an expert in listening to my intuition, thought I knew its voice as well as I knew my native language, English. But I learned that our journeys are complicated, are not always clear, have many layers, and can appear like marquees with bright, shiny lights flashing "This is the way," but that until we dig deeper we don't always know the difference between our ego and our intuition. I learned that I was always learning more and didn't have all the answers—and that was okay. And I learned I was actually intuition's student and it my teacher.

I invite you to learn from my story, to look at your past and ask yourself where you have overidentified with something—an idea, person, place, or job. Look deep into your story and ask yourself, "When have I made decisions from my ego, and when from my intuition?"

Then notice how different your body and spirit feel when you come from a place of truth versus pride.

CHAPTER 14

TRUSTING THAT YOUR INTUITION HAS A PATH OF ITS OWN

*We often forget that we are nature. Nature is not something separate from us.
So when we say that we have lost our connection to nature, we've lost our connection
to ourselves.*

—Andy Goldsworthy

I grew up in Omaha, Nebraska, and every summer we took the same family vacation to one of the five bluest lakes in the world. My fun parents, four siblings, and I would pile into the wood-paneled, baby-blue family station wagon and drive three hours, yet with excited kids, flying Legos, and a fight every fifteen minutes, it felt like thirty hours. We would spend one blissful week in a small white cabin at a resort called Vacation Village, on Lake Okoboji in northwest Iowa. It was a kid's utopia: a week filled with sunburns, swimming, and sand castles, a time to indulge on perfectly cooked cheeseburgers, multiflavored Popsicles, and unlimited pop, which is what we call soda in the Midwest.

When I was in seventh grade, my parents bought a sweet Cape Cod–style cabin on the lake that was all our own. I still visit every summer and now bring my own children and husband to meet my mom, four siblings, their spouses, one niece, and ten nephews to continue this summer tradition of craziness and bliss.

Now that my family lives thousands of miles from Lake Okoboji, we usually fly. But one summer my husband and I had the brilliant, and also kind of crazy, idea of turning our trek to Okoboji into a family road trip. In our two-week adventure, we visited thirty-five friends and family members, frequented twenty-two rest stops, drove through eleven states, and killed only one bird, but that one bird stuck on our front grille for four hundred miles, that poor feathered creature. I thought the highlight of our adventure would be our one week at Lake Okoboji, but what transpired on our return trip home through Bozeman, Montana, was quite unexpected and inspiring.

Bozeman, the home of my sister-in-law's family, was the perfect middle stopping point on I-90 in between two days of driving for thirteen hours each. We had time to rest our worn-out kids and clean out our stinky, crumb-filled, bug-splattered car, and Adam and I could have a beer or two or three and relax after driving and listening to umpteen hours of Harry Potter, which we both secretly loved.

One beautiful morning, Jess and Sharon—my sisters-in-law—Adam, and I were sitting around drinking a strong cup of Montana-brewed coffee and discussing my next book project. I was telling them about my unbelievable interviews and mentioned I wanted to talk to an architect because I felt they had such an intuitive sense of space. Also, each time I am around an architect I notice what deep listeners they are, and I am amazed by how they can look at a blank space and then use their creativity, knowledge, experience, and intuition to create something out of thin air.

Jess's and Sharon's eyes met and their eyebrows rose. "You should interview our friend and architect, Neal," one of them said.

To be honest, at first I was like, "Ah, maybe," but then they shared a bit more of his story, and I instantly heard, "Hell yes." These flickering moments are precious, so I asked, "Can I meet him today?"

Intuitive Guide: Neal

I walked into Neal's modern yet historic home near the Montana State University campus. The first things I noticed were his incredibly warm smile, kind wife, and sweet son. I noticed, too, how Neal was in a wheelchair. As he rolled over to greet me, I experienced warmth throughout my body. I was struck with how comfortable I felt with his mode of transportation. In a split second I was reminded of my father, who, paralyzed on his right side after a stroke, spent the last nine months of life in his wheelchair. After spending so much time with my father in his wheelchair, I have greater comfort with and compassion for people with disabilities.

We proceeded to his backyard, which was scattered with bright neon-green Adirondack chairs and a man-made climbing wall connected to his garage. On this beautiful Montana afternoon I had the honor of hearing Neal's incredible story around intuition, and about how following it saved his body, mind, and spirit.

As Neal began to speak I was fully drawn in by his subtle Southern drawl and strong spirit. Within the first few moments I knew that this interview was going to be about not his intuition as an architect, but his intuition in life.

"When you are being asked a question by a person or life," Neal began, "don't fight it. Follow where the energy is, even if it is in a place you don't want it to be. Just follow the energy. For me intuition is: if there is energy in something or someone, I just say yes."

Neal innately knew to listen to his intuition and say yes to life at a very young age. He was raised four miles from the beach in eastern North Carolina to a stay-at-home mom and banker dad. His adventurous spirit led him to say yes to nature and spend most of his youth surfing and skateboarding; he would spend eight hours a day in the water. He would do anything he could to be outside, so much so his mom would have to drag him away, even after the sun had already set. It was his heaven on earth.

Then in a split second his childhood became not only externally adventurous, but also internally chaotic. When Neal was nine, his parents decided to divorce after a classic but always-painful story of a banker dad having an affair with his secretary. The deceit tore the family apart for some time. "My mom went downhill," Neal shared with me. "My brother, who was sixteen at the time, became my transportation, and I ended up doing a lot of drugs and drinking."

Neal was heading down a destructive path. When he was sixteen, his parents sat him down and told him they were sending him to a family of recovering addicts who ran a wilderness program in Montana called Galena Ridge.

"This was one of the first moments in my life that I really felt my intuition. Because the moment my parents told me I was going to this program, I was like, 'Awesome, this sounds great.' My parents were shocked by my acceptance. You see, I was sixteen, partying; I had a girlfriend. Most kids would be furious, but I just knew deep down that my life was not good and I needed to go to Montana. I left a few days later."

One of the beauties of intuition is this moment of surrender. It is almost unconscious and out of your control, and, as if in a river, you are pulled with the current to your callings. If you go with this flow and let the water take you where you need to go, you will fight less and feel more peace.

Neal's river flowed toward Galena Ridge. In his year and a half there, he not only reconnected to nature, but he also filled the empty part of himself with something besides drugs and alcohol. Because he often had a smile on his face, the couple that ran the program thought he was pulling a fast one on them. They thought he was too happy and were confused because the other kids were so miserable. But Neal loved it there; he surrendered and didn't fight his circumstances and intuitively knew it was the right place for him. At Galena Ridge he turned his life around and learned that Montana was a part of his heart and would always be one of his greatest advocates and teachers.

Soon after leaving Galena Ridge, Neal uncovered another love affair in nature: rock climbing. "There are no rocks where I am from," he said. "When I first came to Montana and saw the majestic mountains and rocks, my imagination went crazy. I asked myself, 'What could I do with it?' Intuition and climbing are similar. When you are climbing, it is like a dance—you are in the flow and in the moment. I am super focused and the most present I have ever been in my life. Because it is so strenuous and relentless, you must be laser focused. When I am climbing, there is something about me and rock and stone. It has nothing to do with the science—I barely survived my geology classes, but always knew the energy of rock was my intuitive passion."

As Neal spoke, the artist Andy Goldsworthy, a British sculptor who has a brilliant way of collaborating with nature and art, popped into my consciousness. "We often forget that we are nature," Goldsworthy said. "Nature is not something separate from us. So when we say that we have lost our connection to nature, we've lost our connection to ourselves." When Neal is in nature, he is one with the rock, sea, or tree. He does not separate himself from the natural elements of the earth. He intuitively knows that to heal his soul he must say yes to nature. When we can all surrender to the fact that we are an integral part of nature, our intuition will open up as wide as the sky.

After Neal's first climb he had a goal to, within a year, climb an extremely challenging route in Kootenai Canyon, the hardest climbing pitch in Montana. He ended up climbing it within ten months. At the time only one other person had ever climbed the route before, and he became Neal's mentor.

Neal's addiction to climbing continued to grow. He wanted to climb even more challenging routes, and in different styles. After he accomplished all these goals, he wanted bigger, more challenging rock, so he traveled to Europe to climb in Chamonix, Fontainebleau, and

Céüse. Neal developed climbing areas throughout North Carolina and Montana, managed climbing shops, and was a rep for climbing gear. Whenever he was asked to do something related to climbing, his gut did not hesitate: "Again, I followed the energy, and I just said yes." Climbing was his whole life. He was at the forefront of the climbing world, with a strong body and loads of talent to back it up.

At the height of Neal's climbing career, he began to hear little intuitive voices that he did not want to listen to. The voices came throughout his body. He tripped over little curbs, lost function in his toes, caught himself on things, and was unable to climb over stairs or lift his foot on climbing holds. The doctors all told him it was a pinched nerve, sent him home with ibuprofen, and told him he would be fine, which gave him an external sense of relief. Internally, however, he knew this was much more than a pinched nerve.

Neal told me about what it was like becoming immobilized: "It became this huge deal and influenced my life in unconscious ways. I started avoiding things. My identity as a climber was affected; I began peeling away from that world, looking for other things to do. I became this crazy cyclist; I could just clip my feet in and go. I would ride a hundred miles on the bike just to get away from what was going on in my head. But I couldn't shake it—cycling never did what climbing did for me. It wasn't as intense. I was twenty-four years old, and intuitively I knew something was wrong, and I was terrified. I thought I had ALS."

Neal then climbed into the world of avoidance, not wanting to face the truth of his situation. This is very common when listening to your intuition. Many times you will not want to listen to what you hear. I have had terrifying moments where I have put in my earplugs of denial in order to believe my life was not going to change. I am sure you can imagine similar times. You are not alone.

"I would run with my girlfriend," Neal continued, "but after a mile I couldn't move my legs anymore and had to lay down and get ice to get any function back. It all hit me like a wall. My girlfriend knew something was up, and so to avoid talking about it, I broke up with her. I didn't want to deal with my life or health."

To continue avoiding these challenging body messages, Neal up and left Missoula with few goodbyes and went back to North Carolina. He visited more doctors, with no answers, and applied to architecture schools. He got accepted to Montana State, and, knowing deep down that his heart was in Montana, he said yes and went back to Bozeman to start his master's program.

Although he continued to hide his condition, Neal's life had become fully altered by his limitations. Instead of climbing, he would fish, or instead of walking across campus with his friends, he would say, "I'll meet you there." He even turned down a job of a lifetime as a mountaineering guide because he knew he could not physically handle the responsibilities. The straw that broke the camel's back was when he had to stop halfway through a ten-day bike tour in Alaska because his body could not finish. He could not hide his condition anymore.

Being the therapist that I am, I asked, "Did you have any total meltdowns, or breaking points?"

Neal looked at me a little confused, which reminded me of the warrior I was talking to, but then he wiggled in his wheelchair and said, "One of my breaking points was one day a guy was trying to be funny, and he tripped me in front of all my friends. I was unable to get back up. I couldn't recover and fell. I knew I couldn't hide my condition anymore."

His health declining, Neal was put through the ringer for a year, going from this doctor to that doctor, doing more and more tests. He finally found the answer to his mysterious health issues with a doctor at the University of Michigan who specialized in a condition called hereditary spastic paraplegia.

Hereditary spastic paraplegia, HSP, is a progressive weakness and spasticity of the legs. Individuals with HSP may eventually require the assistance of a cane, walker, or wheelchair. His disease is in the family of

ALS but only affects Neal's lower extremities. His grandfather had MS, but Neal's case is still mysterious since there are only twenty thousand cases in the United States.

"I have been genetically tested, and nothing correlates with my condition or with my genes," Neal said. "I thought I had ALS; it starts this way. I am not paralyzed. I have sensation in my toes, sixty percent and better as I go up. I can stand with crutches, but I can't move my legs. They don't know if it will get any better."

Because Neal follows the energy of intuition and of saying yes, his mom told him to try Rolfing. Rolfing is an alternative medicine that improves body alignment and movement. Even though he had never tried anything like this before, he felt a yes when his mom suggested Rolfing. He went to an amazing Rolfer and found himself wanting to stay after his appointments to talk to her about life. Thank goodness he did, because that was how he met his wife, Ann.

Ann and Neal had been dating for some time when she told him she was pregnant. Because Neal is someone who realizes that life, like nature, is not a straight line, but curved, intricate, and rough around the edges, he knew they should be together. "I said, 'Awesome, let's do this.' She started crying because she had never felt so supported. I was all in. I said, 'Let's go.'"

I love this story of intuition because it shows the different ways it can come into our lives. Sometimes it is mysterious and quiet, like seeing someone at a coffee shop and feeling as if you should talk to them but you don't know why, or how—you just know. And sometimes it can come in unexpectedly, as it did for Neal. He heard Ann was pregnant, and not one cell in his body questioned whether the two should be together; it was a clear, intuitive yes.

Jackson was born while Neal was in graduate school, a challenging time not only because of the heavy schoolwork, but also because he could no longer hide his disease. This waking-up period was painful.

"One day I went to one of my professors," Neal said. "He was the one I most respected because he came from Harvard, and people were afraid of him. I walked in with a cane. I told him what was going on with me, and he said, 'You might want to look into something else. You need to find another profession. There is a lot of ego underneath architecture, and people will wonder how you are going to get into job sites to get the job completed.' Others were disgusted by what this professor said—it was really harsh—but I wasn't hurt, because I felt the love underneath his message. He still stops by my house."

"Through all this time of disappointment and change, how did you not crumble?" I asked.

"I just needed to move on."

I have intuitively heard these same few words of wisdom: "It is time to move on. You need to move forward into the present and out of the past." Time to transition ahead, these powerful words tell us. No more wallowing in self-pity, in the false narratives we create to keep ourselves safely within our comfort zones. I don't mean to strike a harsh, pull-up-your-bootstraps tone, but there is power in moving forward and not drowning in your past. There is a power in not living in your suffering. Listening to Neal's story, I was reminded that we all have pain, but we can also choose whether to suffer.

After Neal's encounter with the Harvard professor, his professional career not only moved on, but also soared. He earned a graduate degree in architecture, worked at a prestigious and reputable firm, and now has his own architecture firm.

Neal's determination to be active in nature continued as well. He developed a climbing program at Eagle Mount, an adaptive-sports organization in Bozeman. He learned and now teaches how to mono ski, which he is so proud of because it is one of the ways he connects with his son in nature. While you may have thought he had touched and mastered all the elements of nature—rock from climbing, water from surfing, and mountains from skiing—he needed to go even further. He needed to experience the natural element of air. He has found a way to be in a wheelchair and experience air through paragliding.

Years earlier Neal had had a premonition of flying. A friend he was climbing with, one of his biggest supporters, suggested he try hang gliding, saying it was like surfing in the air. Neal remembered having a deep knowing at that moment that flying would be part of his life one day; he just did not know he would be flying in a wheelchair.

He reached out to his friend, who connected him with a man named Chris. Chris was a man of few words. Neal sent him a lengthy email with his story, and Chris replied with "Come down here anytime." Neal asked, "Do I need anything?" Chris simply answered, "Nope."

We talked about how flying can bring up fear for anyone, especially someone in a wheelchair. But Neal intuitively knew flying was for him, because he trusted it and heard a clear yes about it.

"I went to Salt Lake for a week and learned to fly. It was everything I dreamed it would be. I did tandem flights first, with the goal of flying solo. The instructor and I went up to do a tandem flight, he hooked me in, and out of nowhere he said, 'I think you should go alone.'"

Neal's solo flight occurred two weeks before my interview with him. "Intuition is like air," he said, the memory of the flight still fresh on his mind. "You just have to go for it, close your eyes and go."

Trust is such an important aspect to intuition. You may not always 100 percent believe every one of your decisions is going to work out, but can you trust you are doing the right thing? Can you tap into the core of the heart, where trust is nestled, and let go, close your eyes, and fly?

In true Neal fashion, he trusted his intuition, followed the energy, and said, "Let's do it!" He ended up flying for two hours, alone, in a wheelchair through the uninhibited sky.

"I was in tears," he said of his magical flight. "I was so overcome, because for the first time in a long time I felt like the feeling of climbing. When you are up in the air, you are feeling every draft of air. You can feel it one moment, but then you may lose it. You can feel the air going sideways, and frontwards, getting hit with wind elements—you have to be in the moment to deal or you can get into some trouble out there."

Neal closed his eyes, as if he were placing himself back there, suspended in the air. "I found that I was super engaged working with the air like a wave, but it was invisible, so you can't see. I would just close my eyes and feel it and trust."

Neal's sixth sense drew him to paraglide the same way it drew him to architecture and climbing. All three revolve around the same sort of spatial recognition he is attracted to.

"When you were paragliding where did you feel it in your body?" I asked, knowing that intuition lives so much in the body.

He hesitated a bit and appeared taken aback. "I felt it most in my heart. I was so touched by the experience. My moment of flying was a culmination of my life. From meeting my friend while climbing, to now being with Chris, and all they have done for me—they are some of the most kind, loving people I know."

He looked up at me and smiled, likely knowing that I would love his next sentence. "I intuitively knew I was exactly where I needed to be."

A grin grew across my freckled face, not only because he was right—I did love that sentence—but also because I loved his story. With all his ups and downs he chose to not let his fears and worries take him away and never intuitively forgot to say yes, to follow the energy of where he needed to be. Neal reminded me that saying yes is my guiding force to survive my day-to-day life. I must be in my intuition to live a life without anxiety and free from the endless chatter of the mind. Neal did not use his head to make most of his decisions; he followed a place in the center of the body, his heart, that told him "Yes" and "You can do this, and you will survive." He put behind his chatter of the mind and inhibitions of his body to come face to face with his soul.

"I now have big dreams. As my disease progressed, my dreams went down, and I had to get practical. But now that I am flying again, my dreams are huge—not ego dreams. I want to see the world again; I want to do it in the air. I can go to the Alps and see these places again. I thought I would never be in the backcountry again, and now that I am flying, I have these dreams again."

Embracing your intuition allows you to have huge dreams. As you continue to spread your wings further and further, your dreams grow bigger and bigger as well. I see this all the time. Someone will push himself or herself in one direction, conquer a fear, stretch his or her comforts, and have a massive transformation. Afterward they have the courage and wherewithal to dream an even bigger dream. Maybe it started with them traveling to the next town over, then to another state, and finally they had the courage to travel overseas and become, as James Joyce wrote in *A Portrait of the Artist as a Young Man*, "unheeded, happy, and near to the wild heart of life."

As the sun set, I looked over at Neal and shivered with the truth that he had more mobility in his spirit, with a compromised body, than I had in my fully functioning body. I remembered all the times I had complained about a sore muscle, or about not having enough time to fit in a run. All the times I had bitched about how my coffee was not hot enough, or about how I had waited too long to be seated at a restaurant. Neal's story exemplifies the benefits of not labeling something good or bad, right or wrong, but rather placing yourself in the "Neal camp" of "Yes, bring it on. That is awesome." The wise perspective of intuitively knowing that every event in life is part of a larger whole and that if we close down our hearts and get lost in the details, we could miss the whole point of what is happening to us.

We don't know why things happen in this world. Why do people die? Why do things not go the way we want them to go? Why do people struggle with inequality, poverty, or mental illness? Why is there a universal struggle in our society to be seen and heard? Why did an amazing, healthy rock climber contract a disease that limits his mobility and restricts him to a wheelchair? We want to blame God, the environment, or our government. We want to project our tragedies and worries on to other people and institutions so that we don't have to feel the pain of our situation.

Yet I didn't see Neal projecting anything on anyone. He showed me a different side to a challenging situation and gave me hope and perspective. He has the gift of intuitively knowing to follow the energy of his experiences, regardless of whether he is in a wheelchair. In fact, when I asked him if he would have his life any other way, he said no. Neal is teaching us to stay awake and free—to connect to our intuition and say yes to opportunities that come our way.

By saying yes you will build more resiliency and spend less time worrying about what didn't happen and more time connecting to the energy of what is happening. Instead of saying, "Oh, what a tragedy," you will open yourself up to new adventures. And if you wish your life were different, you will hear more clearly which next step your intuition is telling you to take to change your life and set yourself up for your next great success.

I thought I was going to talk to Neal about the intuitive aspects of architecture, and what I ended up learning about was the intuitive gifts of life. Of not getting stuck or paralyzed in our "wheelchairs" of "I can't go do that," "I shouldn't do this," "It cost too much money," or "Others would not approve," and instead saying, "Yes, let's go for it. That is awesome!" A man in a wheelchair with limited movement taught me so much more about moving forward, opening up to my intuition, and not staying stuck in my paralyzed ways of life.

CHAPTER 15

THE AMBIGUITY OF INTUITION

Faith is a passionate intuition.

—William Wordsworth

You will sometimes hear your intuition as clear as a bell. You will not always follow it, but you will not be able to deny that you hear or feel what it is telling you. Then there will be moments when your intuition is not clear; the voice will be confusing and ambiguous, the messages it carries obscure, subtle, cloudy, and not always concrete. Following those messages may lead you down an unknown path, because intuition is not a perfect science or mathematical equation like $1 + 2 = 3$. No, it is more mysterious, which is why it is much easier to follow your logical, controlling mind—and its desire for clear answers, known outcomes, and secure landings—versus your heart.

Intuitive ambiguity may occur when something like ego, jealousy, anger, or resentment comes between you and your heart's desire. Family expectations and societal norms can overshadow your intuition, too. In any case, a cloudy intuition makes following what you know to be true in your heart much more challenging.

Intuitive Guide: Linda

I learned more about the ambiguity of following one's intuition when my family and I were on spring break in San Francisco. We were taking a beautiful walk along the bay toward the Golden Gate Bridge when suddenly a pitter-patter of rain started to slowly fall, and within minutes it turned into a downpour. My husband and I yelled "Run!" to the kids, and we all bolted toward an old airplane hangar nearby. As we entered, we realized—or I should say my kids realized—they had landed in trampoline heaven. The old hangar had been renovated into a trampoline park.

As my kids soared high into the air, contorting their bodies like pretzels, a man and I began with the usual questions of "Where do you live?" and "What is your job?"

"I am a therapist and a writer," I answered.

"Oh," he said, "my girlfriend is a writer, too."

I did not know it at the time, but his girlfriend, Linda, would be my next intuitive guide. She and I began talking, and she shared with me the news of her new book, which was about to be released. As a fellow writer I was ecstatic for Linda and her newly published novel, not an easy thing to come by. I knew she and I would have a lot to talk about regarding life, writing, and intuition.

We both felt the loud trampoline park would not be the best venue to talk about her sixth sense, so we planned on reconnecting over the phone when she returned home. Even with the three-hour time difference, Linda and I found a time to connect. I was thinking we would talk for an hour or so. Was my intuition ever wrong! Linda and I could barely stop chatting. The conversation extended to almost three hours.

Linda was born on the East Coast. Her mom was an artist, her dad an attorney—a nice dichotomy of influences. She felt her clairvoyant gifts from a very young age. When she was seven, her family moved overseas. One vacation, while touring Scottish castles, a strong shiver went up and down her spine. She intuitively felt that there were children buried under the stones of the castle. Later she researched the Scottish castles and found out that her premonition was in fact true.

"As a child, people branded me as weird," Linda told me. "I felt both ostracized and uncomfortable about all that was not talked about and that I knew to be true." She felt she was operating beyond the here and now. She had a deep sense of perception to outside things, a perception she has followed her whole life.

When I asked Linda about intuition, she told me a plethora of stories about her dreams, career, and life. She also mentioned how she was diagnosed with an autoimmune disease. She was so broken down and sick, yet she followed her intuition to get off all the medication and look at her "stuff" in order to find a way to heal. Her disease was a great teacher, she said, because it was easy to learn about life when sick.

After nonstop talking the phone line went quiet for a moment and I wondered if we had gotten disconnected. Then Linda said she wished to go into more depth about her intuition around a relationship.

Linda had lived a vibrant life in New York City for years; she got her master's degree, worked at a major newspaper and broadcast studio, and was an edgy playwright off Broadway. She was successful, on top of the world, never thinking she would leave this alive city that she loved and called home.

Until one day her boyfriend, whom she had been dating for only a short period, asked her to hop in his car and drive across the country with him to Los Angeles. He was moving out there to shoot a TV pilot. Common sense told her not to go. Her logical brain was saying, "You have to work, you cannot afford to travel across the country, and most importantly you have never wanted to go to Los Angeles."

Yet fate took a different turn, and her intuition, albeit somewhat cloudy, softly said, "Go, go, go!"

"There was a part of me that knew I needed to jump in his car and say yes to this call of adventure," Linda said. "I could not hear clearly why, but I deeply knew I needed to go." Again we can see the workings of intuition. Your premonitions may not always be clear and precise, but there is another force at play that is moving you toward the unknown. And in these moments trust is your anchor, the one thing you can count on when your intuitive voice is not as clear as you would wish it to be.

The cross-country journey turned into a life-changing experience. Along the way she and her boyfriend bought rings in a pawnshop and on a lark got married at the Phoenix courthouse, reading their vows from a card printed in both English and Spanish.

"I was not that type of girl to just up and marry someone," Linda was quick to tell me, "and I had no desire to get married at the time." Linda knew from the moment they bought the rings that the marriage was a mistake. "What have you done?" she heard a voice inside her say. "You have to get out of this right now." The nuptials felt more like a movie than real life.

Linda's intuition was blurry at the time, in other words, and complex. Here was a woman who had had a deep presentiment her whole life; since childhood she could hear dead people. This was not her first rodeo. Yet we can be well versed in an area and still sometimes have difficulty tapping into our intuition to make a decision. Even though Linda heard "Do not marry this man" and knew her decision came from the ego and not from the soul, she still proceeded. The choice was neither right nor wrong, necessarily; something in her life merely kept her from thinking or feeling clearly.

Shortly after arriving in Los Angeles her life quickly unraveled. The marriage lasted only seven months. "I had colds that lasted longer than this relationship," she told me. She was in a city she did not feel comfortable in, and she knew very few people.

Yet even during her darkest days, Linda had a flicker of light leading her toward her teachings. The teaching, as unclear as it was at the time, was the voice that said, "Go on this adventure." It was not wrong—it was part of her life journey. She innately knew this short marriage was not about love or a lifelong relationship; it was about venturing into the unknown, and trusting that Los Angeles was exactly where she was supposed to be. Even though she felt lonely, scared, and lost, she knew deep in her bones that LA was her home, but couldn't put into words why. She also trusted in forces outside herself to make the leap, a leap she knew had moved her in the right direction.

Because her marriage ended, some might see Linda's adventure west as a failure, an example of someone mishearing her inner voices or neglecting to listen to her heart. But listening to different voices is not a mistake, and intuition goes beyond right and wrong, success and failure, or good and bad. When your intuition calls you, you can let go of the rules and regulations. You are entering another plane, one without labels or "wrong" consequences. So after you make a decision with your sixth sense, try not to predict or label the outcome or control the situation, because even though the meaning behind your decision might look cloudy, in time you will discover that trusting it was exactly what you needed to do to find your path toward personal growth. A marriage that ended in divorce, for example, may have given you one, two, or twelve beautiful children.

When you recognize that your decisions are not mistakes, you learn to tell the difference between personality and the soul. If you follow your personality, you will go kicking and screaming, and labeling your life in terms of successes and failures, only to be disappointed by your own expectations. If you follow your intuition, you will live from your soul and see your life and circumstances from a much grander point of view.

Linda never shies away from her intuition, even when it compels her to do things she knows might make her life more challenging. "I lean into challenges because I have learned so much from my failures and successes," she said. Her grander view allowed her to have the psychic premonition that her newlywed man and his little, broken-down Honda were the vehicles to get her to Los Angeles and her new life.

To Linda, this was very clear: "Intuition is a psychic premonition. It is about times filled with a deep sense of knowing and pull to do something, even when logic tells you no."

Linda's definition of intuition brought up a very important point: What is the difference between premonition and intuition? Intuition is an umbrella, and underneath this umbrella are the concepts of premonition, déjà vu, lucid or vivid dreams, circumstance, and your sixth sense. Each has intuitive aspects, but they are relayed in different ways. Think of the color red. There are many different shades in the red color scheme—rose, burgundy, and maroon, for instance. Each shade is unique, but all are under the umbrella of red. Premonition is just one shade of intuition.

Linda is not the first person to have committed to an ambiguous gut instinct that may have first appeared to be a mistake but ultimately led to great success. Entertainment icon Jay Z, for example, is known for saying that his days of dealing drugs in the streets, while challenging, were what helped him become such a savvy business mogul. And as a young boy Thomas Edison struggled in school and was told by teachers that he was "Too stupid to learn anything," but these challenges forced him to dig deeper into his soul and build resiliency, and they were the vehicle that drove him toward inventive curiosity and success.

Jay Z and Thomas Edison could only construct these narratives in retrospect, because they could not have possibly known why or how each of their actions would affect their future lives and the lives of others. The same goes with all of us. The cloudiness of intuition is at play each and every day. But if you had a microscope that allowed you to see through the clouds and into the soul, you could observe the beauty that occurs in every situation. You would be able to see the spirit expand from giving money to a homeless person, or from spending time with a loved one as he or she dies. You would see your heart grow deeper to make room for a friend in pain, or to capture your screams as you bring a newborn into this world. When you look back on your life, I am guessing you remember more vividly your challenging experiences than your easy ones, because your challenges molded you into who you are today; they were vehicles for developing your soul.

The problem arises when we begin to put labels on these "soul developers," because labels take away from the life lesson. When we call something right or wrong, or a success or failure, the label influences how we decide whether to continue participating in that part of life and how we let moments from our pasts affect the present and future. For example, notice how you feel when you hear these activities: going to church, doing drugs, staying faithful to your spouse, or missing one of your kid's soccer games. What comes up for you? Do you feel guilt, excitement, fear, or shame? So often you can put dogmas, rules, and regulations on your life that inhibit you from fully expressing your intuition.

I am not saying that everyone should go out into the world and do whatever they want. No, I am smarter than that—and so are you. We have speed limits and laws to keep us safe for a reason. As a therapist I know the value of boundaries and staying grounded, safe, and stable. What I am saying is that when you label something within those boundaries as right or wrong, you are putting a barricade around your intuition.

I heard an author talking about these exact barricades. Her book was about her marriage and her husband's infidelity. While writing the book, she learned that it did not matter if she stayed or left the marriage. What mattered was the voice inside her that, if she were honest and still enough, would tell her what to do next: to stay or go. Listening to this voice, she knows she won't betray herself ever again. As long as her still, small voice tells her to stay in the marriage, she will stay, and the second it tells her to go, she will go, and she is not afraid anymore of either outcome because she has learned to trust the voice and to trust herself.

If you wholeheartedly trust your still, soft, wise voice—without letting fear drown it out or overrule it, and without worrying about the outcome—you will keep yourself from placing caution signs around your decisions and you will allow all the vehicles of intuition to bring beauty into your life. Linda is our intuitive guide here for this very reason. Her voice said, "Go," and she went; that voice was the vehicle that changed her life forever.

"I had to believe that there was something so much bigger than myself," Linda said. "I had to surrender to what I was hearing from God. This was a God shout. God was speaking through me to drop everything."

Begin to listen to your "God shouts" of intuition and trust them, rely on them, and let them be your guides. Linda's story reflects the reality that things don't always look the way they seem. Some things may not work out, which often compels us to jump into a place of shame: "What is my problem—why did I marry that person?" or "What was I thinking—how could have I been so stupid to have taken that job?" But what if we can begin to look at these life choices not as mistakes, but as opportunities to learn? Can you embrace the notion that your intuitive voices and life are not always going to be clear? Can you trust that you are not always in control, driving the car of your life, but simply a passenger looking out the windows? And can you trust that you will be okay regardless of what happens? In ambiguity we often learn our deepest lessons.

The cloudiness of intuition, and real rain clouds, led me to that trampoline park and to Linda that day along San Francisco Bay. Linda's story reminds us to follow our gut feelings, against all the odds, even though it may not always appear clear or as if it is leading you to the right place. You may not see the benefits of doing so until the future—weeks, months, even years later—but this truth you hear will arrive. In the meantime, try to discover a place deep inside your being where you can retreat to when you are uncertain or afraid. Focus on something that brings you peace, and use the techniques I have mentioned throughout this book to help you trust that this too shall pass. If you can be patient, have faith, and let go, you will find that your true calling has brought you home.

CHAPTER 16

STANDING IN THE UNIQUENESS OF YOUR INTUITION

The things that make me different are the things that make me me.

—A. A. Milne

Most of us have asked ourselves, "Who am I?" and "What am I passionate about?" and "How do I want to leave this world?"— deep questions that help awaken us to our intuitive voices and learn about how we listen, talk, instruct, inspire, and motivate ourselves. Waking up to our sixth sense also helps us peel away the layers of the self to discover which gifts and talents make each of us unique, whether it be culinary genius, a creative spirit, computer skills, or anything else.

My next intuitive guide, Cindy Elkins, has discovered what makes her unique—she is an "N of 1," she told me—by following her callings and believing in her intuitive voice. The clinical-trial term N of 1 was new to my vocabulary. Typically, a clinical trial has many participants— that is, an N of 100 or N of 1,000, where the N stands for "number," as in the number of individuals in the sample size. An N of 1 is a clinical trial in which a single patient is the entire trial, a single case study. It's about studying one participant for the greater good of the entire study. By doing this introspective work on the one, all benefit.

To be an N of 1 means that you don't have anyone to measure your success against, because no one has ever walked the road you are walking. For example, Hillary Clinton became the first woman to be a major-party nominee for president of the United States, making her an N of 1.

To reap the benefits of a whole, authentic N of 1 mind-set, you must first know yourself. You must spend time alone tapping into your intuitive spirit, your north star, your inner light. Only then will you build confidence in your passions, make bolder decisions, and take more risks. Further, you will develop authentic connections with family, friends, and colleagues, so for the greater good of humanity it is beneficial that we all understand our "self"—our drives, passions, and interests—because doing so is contagious and helps ensure everyone realizes they are an N of 1, too.

Intuitive Guide: Cindy Elkins

Cindy Elkins was a high-level executive at a $43.7 billion biotech company. She is one of the 11 percent of women in the male-dominated world of Silicon Valley. Being the only woman in the room is not new for Cindy; her intuitive calling of being an N of 1 has been with her since childhood.

Childhood

Cindy was born in Albuquerque, New Mexico. Her parents had her when they were students at the University of New Mexico, when her mom was eighteen and her dad twenty. Her father was a top salesman for Control Data, the Google or Facebook of its time. With her father's job Cindy moved around a lot as a child. They lived in New Mexico, Texas, Minnesota, Southern California, and Northern California. "I grew up watching my dad at the data center," she said. "He was the most brilliant salesperson. I often say I am second-generation technology. To be a part of a lineage of high tech is unique."

Her mother was a stay-at-home mom whose focus and dedication to Cindy's well-being helped her develop her N of 1. Her parents supported her north star and inner light so that she could hear her true callings around her passions and interests and develop into a curious, independent, confident person at a very young age.

Cindy's parents were not the only ones who helped develop her inner knowing. An only child, she also grew during her time alone. Cindy came of age in an era when the average family meant having three children, so being an only child was her first experience as an N of 1. When she was not with her imaginary friend Jarfus, she was alone playing Monopoly or any board game she could get her hands on. I asked her if she was ever lonely as a child. "No," she instantly said. "I enjoyed being alone, and my parents were so young when they had me, it was as if we were all growing up together." This early development of introspection gave Cindy time to explore who she was. One thing she intuitively discovered was that she loved spending time not with all the neighborhood kids, but with her maternal grandmother, Evelyn, with whom she had a unique and close relationship.

From the age of five Cindy would fly to Albuquerque to spend the summers with her grandma. Evelyn was an amazingly strong woman. She grew up in a small town in Texas with her entire extended family, and she was the first of them to leave and move to Dallas. And because her husband was in the military, she ended up traveling all over the world. Fiercely independent, Evelyn played a monumental part in forming Cindy's character. Their relationship laid the foundation for Cindy to nurture her intuition, believe in herself, and stand up for what she believed in. Evelyn's independent life also showed Cindy how to be an N of 1, to not shy away from the voices telling her it was okay to be different or to stand out.

Cindy always knew she had a strong intuition. "On the night my grandma died, I was unable to be with her, but my mom was with her. In the middle of the night, I literally shot out of bed, looked at the clock, and then saw three huge flashes of light. I knew in my heart she had died. I talked to my mom the next morning and asked, 'What time did Grandma go?' and she told me it was nearly the exact time I saw the flashes of light."

As Cindy told me this story over Skype, I became aware I was witnessing a very intimate moment: an incredibly strong, successful woman, who lives in a world of left brain and technology, had tears in her eyes. Sometimes when the heart is touched, tears are contagious, so I teared up as well. Cindy got where she is today because of her intelligence, drive, and competitive spirit, but also because her childhood gave her the heart and the confidence to listen to internal validation versus only external. Evelyn's guiding force still helps her embrace being an N of 1.

Cindy has also embraced being an N of 1 in her love of sports. When she was in fourth grade, her parents signed her up to play basketball in the small town of Irving, Texas. At that time there were very few girls playing sports, and because the male coaches did not feel the girls would be able to run the whole basketball court, Cindy's team played on only half of it—the first of many biases Cindy would face as a woman in a man's world. But she found her competitive spirit anyway. Nobody was going to tell her how she could succeed in sports or life. "I love team sports," she went on to tell me. "I love the feeling of winning, leading teams, and doing things that most folks would say are impossible."

Her words remind me of another voice of intuition: the voice of strength. The voice of strength sounds like "Tell me I can't do something, and then watch out!" When you hear this voice of determination, which gives you the strength to go against the grain or stand up to the biases or the impossible, listen deeply—it is part of your soul's code.

"This attitude of doing things that most folks would say were impossible also led me to my love of math," Cindy said. Even though girls start to lose interest in math when they are fifteen on average, according to a survey commissioned by Microsoft, Cindy's passion did not wane. "It was math that taught me I have always been an N of 1."

Cindy was quite often one of few girls, and then women, in her math classes. She embodied the mathematical concept of an N of 1 at UCLA as an applied-math major. "Math is a fascinating language. It is what taught me to look at things very logically, and how to break things up in chunks and process different parts. It is an art. It shaped my ability to think about how to attack different opportunities and look at a problem. . . . Even today I sit in a meeting, look around, and I can count the low number of women in the room and figure out the percentage. And then I ask myself, 'There are still not a lot of us, and why?'"

As she spoke about the inequality of women, I experienced a pain in my chest, almost like a muscle strain in my heart. I realized I was somatically feeling the continued bias that girls and women still face today. Women make only 77 cents for every dollar that men earn, four in ten businesses have no women in senior management, and male athletes receive $183 million more in athletic scholarships each year than females do. This is just not right. Cindy is an N of 1 in women's rights as well. She sets an example for all girls and woman to follow their intuition and to fight like a warrior for their gifts and talents, especially when faced with judgment based on gender.

Was it a fluke, or did Cindy intuitively feel my pain? Because she then said, "I continue to be very passionate about math for my twelve-year-old twin girls. I want them to love math as much as I do and overcome the built-in bias against girls in STEM programs. I am very acutely aware of getting more girls and women involved in science and math, and I believe it starts at home with me and my partner and our girls." The moment she finished this sentence my pain dissolved. Not because I think she is going to solve all the problems around women's rights, but because in her heart she is trying to make a difference.

Personal Life

You would think that growing up an only child, being the only girl drawn to math when other girls her age were drawn to boys, or playing sports in a town where very few girls did would be enough to help Cindy define who she is and why she is on this planet. But little did she know that one of her most defining "Who am I?" moments was still to come.

When Cindy was a teen, she realized she was gay. She knew at the time she could not come to terms with her sexuality and continued dating boys. In her early thirties she knew she had to be honest with her life. Even so, she was still in a bit of disbelief and in this instance didn't want to be an N of 1. Frustrated, she would say to herself, "Really, come on. I know myself very well on a deep level of introspection. I have to go deeper?"

I often see intuitive questioning like this from clients faced with a life challenge, whether it is around their sexuality, marriage, children, or health. They are forced to truly awaken to their being, to walk another journey, to have their feet in the fire, and to turn yet another chapter in the book of their lives. Cindy walked this walk, doing it the best way she knew how—in her intuition and soul, alone. She moved out of a house she shared with her best friend and roommate, got a condominium alone, dropped off the grid, and took twelve to eighteen months to find out who she was. Her friends still kid her about taking some of that time to read Dante's *Inferno*. "I had to search my soul so deeply. And from this experience I heard my true voice come through, and this is what it told me: 'Cindy, this is who you are, and you must live your life authentically, with full integrity.' I can guarantee you I have discovered so much more about myself because of this deep reflection." Shortly after this soul-searching, Cindy met her partner, and they have been together for eighteen years.

Our conversation continued, and I asked, "Can you tell me more about how your intuition has played a part in your life?"

"My intuition comes to me in interesting ways," she said. "I have a beautiful bougainvillea tree, and I said to myself, 'I hate to think what our patio would be like without that magnificent tree.' A few months later it died. Or I was writing an important email to someone and thought, 'No, I don't like how that sounds. It's not time yet.' The next day the person I was sending the email to sent me an email. I totally believe in a connected unconsciousness of our humanity. And each time it happens to me, I ask myself, 'Well, you knew, and you had a good inkling that was happening—why do you dismiss it? Why do you keep saying that doesn't mean anything?'"

We looked at each other, knowing we were kindred spirits who believed in humanity's collective unconsciousness, and the deep importance of this concept for all human beings.

Career

When I asked Cindy about her career, she spent a few moments humbly rattling off her incredibly impressive résumé with experience at different tech companies as a software developer, project leader, manager, senior director, and vice president. She shared a lot of acronyms such as P&L, CIT, or B2B, some of which I needed to google quickly as she was talking in hopes of not looking ignorant in our current tech world.

"I finally landed at Genentech," Cindy said, "which was fascinating because one of the biggest drugs we were working on at the time was for wet, age-related macular-degeneration disease. It was amazing because it was this disease that ultimately took my grandma's eyesight. It has been a wonderful company, and my family has always been so proud of me, but the one thing I am most proud of is when people ask me what I do, I can say, 'I get to help people like my grandma.' It means a lot. So often in the tech world it's not a mission-based company. But in Genentech's case they will leave the world a better place."

Cindy paused, then began speaking about how her intuition had affected her career "I often get asked the question, 'Did you know you were going to be this one day?' And I say, 'I just follow what I feel; I tap into what is going on in our organization, and what is being asked of me. Then I ask myself, "What am I prepared to give? What do I believe is the next best thing to do? And how do I guide and lead this team and community?" Then I have these moments when I hear from my inner voice, "You know what to do next." It forces me to tap into my intuition.'"

Cindy went on to say she also listens wholeheartedly to her intuition when hiring her team. "Is this a good person?" Cindy said she would ask herself. "Do they have a high level of integrity? How do I feel when I am with them? I am very observant and listen intently, and that informs my inner voice. I am constantly trying to figure out, 'Do I believe in this person? Do I believe in what they are saying about this company? Would I trust them with my future? With my heart and soul?' From asking these questions I can usually get a hit on somebody very rapidly. When I fight my first intuition on a person and allow my head to beat up my gut, it usually ends up poorly. I can then get myself into a pickle. I must follow my intuition."

Cindy, like Peter, knows there are some defining moments in her career, one being that listening to her inner voice can set her trajectory for success. "When I joined Genentech, my boss had already started an amazing program around the head-heart-body connection. It incorporated mindfulness and meditation to create a holistic development program." By participating in these programs, Cindy learned how to home in on her intuition and realized the importance of having this mindfulness practice in the tech industry.

Then sadly her beloved boss decided to move on. After he left, the team had an identity crisis. He was charismatic and left a big hole during a fragile and transitional time for the company. When her boss moved on, Cindy became the team leader. She realized there was a moment when the whole team could have disappeared as a group, culture, and community. Cindy knew she could not be their old boss; she needed to be herself. And by revisiting the "Who am I?" question, she reconnected to the importance of being an N of 1 leader.

"I heard an inner voice that said, 'Here are some questions we each need to answer together to really anchor us. Why are you here? What are you passionate about? And who are you?'" A huge grin spread across Cindy's face. "One of my favorite books is *Alice in Wonderland*. I love this book, especially when the Cheshire Cat asks Alice, 'Who are you?' I thought to myself, 'We need to each answer this question, who am I? An interesting question—with three words, and three letters in each word— because if we don't know who we are, we have no chance in gathering everyone's hearts again and leading us through this transition successfully.'"

My whole body was buzzing, because this question is pivotal to tapping into one's intuition. "Who am I?" is one of the most important questions you can ask yourself. Mystics and sages, political leaders and philosophers have been asking themselves it for centuries. This inquisition can help you discover your own identity, passions, and purpose by helping you clear away your chaotic thoughts, leading you to the core of your soul. If there was one question you could ask yourself to hear, feel, and experience your gold mine of intuition, it is "Who am I?"

I am reminded of two occasions when this introspective question changed and impacted someone's life. The first was when a friend of mine, who is eighty, has lived all over the world, and has been married three times, told me that "Who am I?" is the first thing she asks herself as she wakes up every morning. And the second is from Paulo Coelho, author of the book *The Alchemist*, who said in an interview that the driving question behind all his writing is "Who am I?" "I find myself a different person," he said. "I'm always a mystery to myself. If I knew in the first hours of the morning what I'm going to do, what is going to happen, what attitude or decision should I take—I think my life would be deadly boring because, well, what makes life interesting is the unknown. It is the risks that we take every single moment of a single day."

Cindy knew that this "Who am I?" question would be the bond that held her team together during this transitional, mysterious time. The next question Cindy's inner voice told her to ask her team was "What are you passionate about?" She told her team to figure out what they were passionate about and share that with each other. "I am all about living out loud," Cindy said.

Cindy learned about living out loud as a young child with her grandma. "My grandma and I would sit on her couch, and if we were approaching a tough topic, she would say to me, 'I'll be Frank and you be Ernest.' She also learned about living out loud from coming out as a gay woman. "From being gay, I discovered as a leader I must live more openly, with integrity, and it was super important for me to have this one phrase integrated into our team: say it out loud."

"Say it out loud" was yet another example of Cindy being an N of 1. Her leadership skills—encouraging her team to speak up, shout out, open up, be honest, and tell the truth—are rare in large organizations.

During the conversation I had a flashback of a friend who told me a story about how when she was working at a large marketing firm, she was the only woman on the executive team, where she was not encouraged to say it out loud. She was fighting for a campaign she truly believed in. Her male boss pulled her aside after one of their group meetings and said, "Can you be a little softer?" Hers is not the only story I have heard of a woman told by her male boss to "Be softer," "Be quieter," or "Be more feminine." Cindy's "Say it out loud" approach is rare and courageous, and most importantly it creates a culture of honesty and intuition for all. When you can say it out loud, you are essentially speaking from your heart.

Two amazing moments at the office helped Cindy's team believe that she meant it when she said they could say it out loud. During an all-hands meeting, Cindy said, "We've built a culture of accountability, integrity, courage, passion, and trust together, so it's okay to ask me anything." One man stood up and said, "We have been through a lot. I think we all want to know: Are you going to stay at the company and with us?" "The whole room stopped, and I stopped," Cindy told me. "And I was very aware to not say something that sounded trite, like I was going to stay forever. . . . I simply said, 'I think you asked the question in the bubble over everyone's head. I'm going through the same thing you all are going through. I love the mission of this company, and I think I am the leader and up to the task, and yes, I am going to stay.' Those are the moments where folks believe you as a leader, because you say it out loud."

What Cindy had done in that meeting was so powerful and therapeutic. Her answer to his question did not matter; what mattered was that she gave him the space to speak his truth. Cindy created an environment of openness without fear and shame. Saying it out loud is revolutionary. How I wish companies, cultures, and communities would implement this concept in order to pollinate intuition and let it grow.

Community

After three years creating a thriving community where everyone could bring their best selves to work every day, Cindy began to see signs of entitlement in the culture and community. So in 2015, she and a key team leader developed an annual theme they called Attitude of Gratitude. They wanted to reanchor the team in all that was good by having everyone remember how fortunate they were to be able to support the scientists and help the company discover, develop, manufacture, and make available medicines for unmet medical needs. Through all the years of mindfulness, well-being, and whole-person development, it was Attitude of Gratitude that resonated the deepest for the whole community. Cindy intuitively knew that the community was prepared to dive that much deeper into the topic.

Being an N of 1 is about going against the grain, beating the odds, and changing the statistics, to the betterment of all people. Knowing this, Cindy found another way to embrace her role as an N of 1—in the corporate boardroom. She had presented to boards before and had prepared slide decks for others to present to boards, so she had always been curious about what happened behind those boardroom doors. Being that women today only hold 19.2 percent of board seats on companies in the S&P 500 index, Cindy's mission was not surprising: "I wanted to be an even better role model for my daughters. I wanted to do something that was statistically improbable to get done, and I wanted my daughters to hear from their mom about being in a boardroom, or meeting with the chairman of the board."

In the process of obtaining a board seat, Cindy continued to listen to her still, small voice of intuition. She began by doing what she does best: talking with people, asking questions, and being an active listener. She described herself as a "personal introvert and professional extrovert," a combination of traits that allowed her to discover many answers to her questions about being on a board.

One day she received an email about a board opportunity at Weight Watchers. Cindy instinctually felt interested and excited but was not sure of the correct protocol to acquire a seat. Did she need a résumé, references? Who did she need to talk to? She ended up meeting with the board, the chairman, and the CEO of Weight Watchers and was confirmed for a seat in 2014.

"My intuition played a big part in this process. I am very passionate about the Weight Watchers mission because it helps people change their lives. My mom grew up having a difficult relationship with food and her own weight-loss journey. I have a lot of empathy for what people are going through, and Weight Watchers' mission is a noble intersection of science, community, and technology. While deciding to take the board seat, the voice in my head kept saying, 'What an amazing journey this is going to be. It is going to be a good thing with great people, and with a mission you love.'"

Cindy told me it has indeed been a phenomenal experience to be on the board with some very accomplished women. In late 2015 Oprah Winfrey joined the Weight Watchers board, and Cindy, originally the only woman on the board, went from being an N of 1 to an N of 2. "I went quite a different route of obtaining my board seat at Weight Watchers. Instead of following what you might read in blogs or hear at a conference, I followed my intuition and my passion."

We were running short of time, so I asked Cindy, "What else would you want to share?"

"Attitude of Gratitude and 'Say it out loud' are all about that higher calling and telling the truth. When I am in my integrity, I cannot lie—I have a hard time. Intuition goes with integrity, and I have to ask myself, 'Am I really going to lie to myself? Why would I do that?' As a leader I want to give my team permission to say it out loud. As a leader I try to tap into my inner voice or my intuition that has proven to be quite wise over the years."

She paused for a moment. "I have a name for my inner critic—it is Sylvia. And I have a name for my inner superhero—it is my grandma's name, Evelyn. I ask myself, 'What is Sylvia saying, and what is Evelyn saying?' I have to trust my superhero—my grandma's voice—enough to let it be my guide. So far it has worked out. To be a leader in a science-based company and in high tech, it is usually fact, fact, fact, data, data, data, and here I am leading through the heart. I am leading through passion, I am leading through trust, and I am leading through being an N of 1."

I began to shake a bit, and chills ran up and down my spine, because as an intuitive guide Cindy recognizes the gift of being alone in order to tap into intuition, then using the wisdom from that voice to create a culture of oneness, universality, and cohesiveness. Her heart is filled with desire to contribute to the greater good, be that for female athletes, girls and women in math, anyone coming to terms with his or her sexuality, or women leading a team in a culture of men. Cindy follows that wise voice she has heard since childhood and continues to hear with the blessing of her grandma, the voice that encourages her to make her mark on this world by being an N of 1.

CHAPTER 17

THE INTUITION OF SELF-ACCEPTANCE

Forgiveness means I've stopped wishing that things would have gone differently.
Forgiveness means I've begun moving forward with my heart open and light, rather
than closed and dark.

—*Elena Brower*

After working with families and children for over twenty years, I would say the most prominent theme I see is the yearning for self-acceptance. The desire to love oneself wholeheartedly, to accept our cellulite and calluses, to embrace our perceived imperfections and beautiful humanness. I have witnessed immense pain from clients worrying about how well they did on an exam or project or in a sporting event. And unending amounts of energy exuded over the inner critics' voices asking, "Am I good enough, smart enough, pretty enough, skinny enough, and safe enough to exist in this world?"

Self-acceptance is about not questioning what the heart knows to be true. It is about not believing all the stories you tell yourself that make you feel as if you are failing in life. It is about not regretting the past or worrying about the future, but striving to stay in the present moment, because in the present you will intuitively feel that you are truly loved, adored, and accepted.

There is energy you instantly experience the moment you meet someone who encompasses the essence of self-acceptance. You can feel their essence of self-love through their confident words and grounded body language.

Intuitive Guides: Suzanne and Jenny

One gorgeous Sunday in July I headed to a small alleyway café to work. I ordered my chai tea, sat down, and began to write, but I was having a hard time getting settled. My body could not get comfortable on the wooden bench, and, wiggling around, I spilled my tea all over my shirt. As I got up to grab some napkins, I felt a pull in my gut to stop and look over my shoulder. I saw a mother and daughter sitting toward the back of the café on an old leather couch. Their hands were entwined, and the daughter was taking a nap on her mother's shoulder. I instantly knew I needed to talk to them about intuition.

Could I have had this premonition because the mother appeared calm while she lovingly embraced her sleeping daughter? Or was it the distinctive and soft features of a daughter who has Down syndrome? I began to walk toward them in an intuitive trance.

The mother greeted me with a smile that would make you think we had known each other for years. I greeted her with my name and dove into my spiel about how I was writing a book on intuition and that something told me I had to walk over to meet her. The mother introduced herself as Suzanne and her daughter as Jenny. The moment Suzanne began to speak, I felt she had some inner knowing into the secret world of intuition.

"I am a mother of three girls," she said. "My first two pregnancies were totally within the bell curve and very normal. But from the beginning of my third pregnancy, with Jenny, I felt as if something was different. It was a sheer gut feeling—I had no evidence."

She spoke calmly so as to not wake Jenny. "I just intuitively knew something was not the same. All the routine tests came out fine—the ultrasounds detected nothing unusual, and there were no concerns raised by the doctors—but I felt in my gut that something was different. It was nothing but my intuition at work."

One of the gifts of intuition is its ability to understand something without the need for conscious reasoning, to know something before you really know it.

Jenny stirred a bit, and Suzanne patted her leg with a deep love. "In utero, she was a really active baby, and her activity level was different. I know this sounds funny, but it was less organized and coordinated. . . . When I was in labor, we packed our bags, got our childcare lined up, and were heading out to the hospital. That whole journey I felt nervous, not nervous excitement, but nervous for the big change that was coming. It was not a feeling of fear or foreboding; it was a deep knowing that this birth and this child were going to change our lives."

Jenny began to stretch. It was almost as if her intuition, hearing her mom's last sentence, knew to wake her. I found myself unusually excited to meet this seventeen-year-old. Jenny awoke with a warm smile and calmness similar to her mother's. She kept holding her mother's hand, and I felt their unconditional love.

Suzanne looked at her daughter and met her with a smile "During labor," she continued, "I could not wear contact lenses and did not have my glasses. Because of this, the moment she was born I could not quite see her. As they handed Jenny to me, I gasped and my first thought was 'She is beautiful.' And then the room went silent. At this moment time stopped and I could see something in her that the other people could not see, an inner and outer beauty. . . . I wish I could have held on to that moment of clarity and relief for a bit longer." She told me she remembered thinking that regardless of the circumstances, "it's all okay. So what if [life] is going to change? She is perfect."

Precious moments like these represent intuition at its core. The world freezes, nothing outside matters, and you see life, people, and all situations as beautiful, real, and fully alive.

"This euphoric feeling only lasted a few minutes. Since Jenny's condition was not predicted, doctors and specialists rushed into the room, and the energy completely changed. I now realize kids with Down syndrome from ages zero to two have multiple appointments with specialists and can have complications. It is a constant experience of someone else putting fear into you."

She realized that if she had known about Jenny's disability while pregnant, her experience and emotions about the pregnancy, labor, and birth naturally would have changed. But because she did not know, she was able to attach to her daughter without fear or worry but simply with love. If you could attach to all people just with love, how different would your relationships be? "If you can just hold the baby in your arms," Suzanne told me, "all fears go away and your instinct and intuition take over."

When you are coming from a place of intuition and trust instead of fear and control, you too will be more present and able to appreciate each and every moment.

Suzanne stayed calm and grounded during this trying time by meditating, something she had done since childhood.

"Does Jenny meditate?" I asked.

"She has her own Zen going on, right, Jenny?"

Jenny smiled. "Right."

We began discussing the role of a parent of a child with a disability. "Does this affect your intuition?" I asked.

"Being a parent to a child with a disability, intuition is a necessity," she said. "You have to be able to read what your child needs before they need it. It's about learning how to pick up on the little signals while paying attention to their every emotion. Intuition to me is the same way. I need to be intuitive to the little signals, such as knowing the difference between an excited gaze versus a tired gaze. I instinctively watch what soothes Jenny, and then I offer that to her. Jenny would oftentimes be understimulated, so we needed to find things to perk her up. Musicals are her thing. Children with Down syndrome are not going to tell you or seek it out themselves, and that is why intuition is monumental. This is where I have learned to make it a priority in my life, in order to be the best mother I can be."

That statement illuminated my heart, not only because it confirmed my hypothesis that intuition is necessary to enhance self-acceptance, but also because I loved hearing how Suzanne found a beautiful, authentic, emotional way to truly connect to her daughter. Because she has a child with Down syndrome, she is forced to live in her intuition. What a gift. She cannot question its power or existence, because she must rely on it every day to connect and communicate with her daughter.

Think if we all lived this way, if we used our intuition to connect with people and didn't question its validity. We could simply trust that it was real and was one of the best methods for living well. Think how beautiful our relationships would become.

"My intuition also comes up with pragmatic solutions to help my family and to have my life run smoothly," Suzanne continued. "Since having Jenny I have developed more intuitions about all people and pragmatic solutions."

I asked Suzanne about Jenny's intuition.

"Jenny has an intuition in that she can spot someone on the spectrum from a mile away." When Jenny heard this, she leaned over and kissed her mom. "She has an open heart. One of the characteristics of kids with Down syndrome is they have excellent people skills. Their auditory memory skills may be poor, but their social skills are beyond age level. And since social skills can be a challenge for kids on the spectrum, Jenny has an intuitive way of spotting this difference."

As Suzanne was talking, Jenny kept looking over at her mom and saying, "I love you, Mom. I love you, Mom."

"You are a special girl, aren't you?" Suzanne replied.

As Jenny heard these heartfelt words, her whole essence melted into her mom's body. "Yes, I am," she responded with total confidence.

At that moment I knew with every bone in my body that this was what a mother-daughter relationship should look like. When both have a relationship in the heart, they will inevitably have a deeper connection. They don't let rules or expectations such as "You need to wear this" or "You need to eat that" get in the way. No, it comes down to "I love you, Mom" and "You are a special girl." It is that simple. We complicate relationships, especially as parents. We worry so much about having our kids do, be, and say the perfect thing that we forget to simply let our intuition and love be our driving forces.

I could tell Jenny was getting restless, and I was reminded that I had only met Suzanne thirty minutes before. I thought I should probably let them get on with their day, but I had one more question. "What have you learned from this experience?"

"This is what I have learned living with Jenny," Suzanne said. "People always say, 'If you have a child with a disability, they will always love you.' But what she has taught me is not that she will always love me, but how much she loves herself. I learn so much from that deep love Jenny has for herself. It is so hard for us to accept that position of always loving ourselves. She will wake up with crusty eyes and crazy hair, but she will look into her mirror, toss her hair to one side, and say, 'Perfect.'"

Jenny then repeated "Perfect" in her soft, angelic voice.

"This is such an example for me," Suzanne continued. "And when you see this at the right time, you think to yourself, 'I am not going to hate on myself today. I am going to do the best to be like Jenny today, toss my faults to the side.'"

Jenny's eyes were wide open, and Suzanne asked herself, "What was I afraid of? Nothing. I just knew there was a great change coming.

When you are feeling low, do like Jenny does and when you pass a mirror blow yourself a kiss on your way out the door and say, 'Perfect.'"

Suzanne's story was a gift from the gods. I am not blinded—I am sure there are many challenging, imperfect days for her and Jenny—but overall there are so many more blessings.

That day at the café I got to see a beautiful, intuitive relationship in action. When Jenny wanted to sleep for an hour in a public café, she slept. When Jenny wanted to give her mom a kiss, she did not worry about what others would think; she simply reached over and planted one on her mom's cheek. When Jenny wanted to say "perfect" about the way she looked, she didn't question her appearance, ego, or body image; she intuitively said, "Perfect." Jenny felt into her instincts and deep callings and without hesitation followed their wisdom toward total love and self-acceptance.

Suzanne has followed her daughter's wisdom with insight. She learned how to tap into her sixth sense so that she would know when Jenny may need something, from a hug to a homemade sandwich. She has made intuition a priority in order to communicate with her daughter and has trusted her gut instincts in order to feel what emotions Jenny may be feeling and address those emotions at any moment. Suzanne learned how to feel into her own body in order to best support Jenny's body as well.

Suzanne did not choose to implement intuition into her life; it just came one day when she looked into her new baby's eyes, gasped, and said, "Beautiful."

When we are in a state of self-love, we are really in our intuition. When we are in a place of self-acceptance, we are in our spiritual power. All of us have the ability to feel this "perfect." If we sit quietly with ourselves, we will hear that we are in God's hands. We will deeply know that we are taken care of and loved fully. When we make intuition a priority in our lives, we make self-love a priority, too. And from this place, anything is possible.

I started that day a bit frustrated because I would have rather not been inside on a beautiful Sunday afternoon. I look back and am so thankful that one of my intuitive decisions was to go write in a café and have the pleasure of meeting Suzanne and Jenny. Because I decided to follow my own heart, not only did I learn so much about intuition, but my day was simply "perfect," too.

CHAPTER 18

The Ultimate Place of Intuition: Love

In the end these things matter most: How well did you love? How fully did you live? How deeply did you let go?

—Jack Kornfield

Since you began this book, you have ventured—emotionally, spiritually, and physically—to dig down deep into the core of your being and unearth that inner voice, your intuition. You have learned from our intuitive guides that in order to find, listen to, and act upon the wisdom from that voice—and to do so often—you must first set a foundation, one built of several key ingredients: being present, distinguishing your one true voice from among many others competing inside you, advocating for yourself and others, waking up to all your bodily sensations, and recognizing that this sixth sense of yours can come in many different forms.

To turn the intuitive house that you have built upon this foundation into a home, however, you need one more ingredient. You need love.

Love is everywhere. The Sufi poet Rumi wrote, "Love is the bridge between you and everything." I encourage you to open your eyes and take a moment right now to look around you. What do you see if you look with your heart, not your hurt? What do you see if you gaze with gratitude instead of greediness? What do you see if you look with grace for all human beings, not just one human being? You see love.

You see love in a child's sparkling, innocent eyes, contagious giggles, and joie de vivre. You feel love in nature's quiet heartbeat of the trees, ancient wisdom of the land, and the warmth of the sun that creates life in a budded flower. And if you look deep, you can even see love in your heartache, when you lost someone dear to you, got fired, or were thrown in jail or out of your house. You can also see love when someone hurts you or you hurt someone. You can see love in your darkest days of depression, and in your manic moments. And you can see love as a catalyst for change, or as a plow that clears your garden of resentment, fear, jealousy, and rage. If you crack open your heart to all that is around you, you can see love in everything, absolutely everything.

How do you create this magical place of love and self-love that turns your intuitive house into a home, into a sacred space where you do not betray yourself or censor your one true voice?

You must first develop greater self-worth, which means embracing all of yourself—your light and your dark, your prizes and pimples, your awards and atrocities. Then you must practice love every day. Make it part of your schedule. It can be big or small, and directed at either yourself or others—saying hello to a stranger, dropping off a gift for a friend, or just having a cup of coffee, receiving a massage, or telling yourself a self-love message like "I know life is really hard right now, but hold on to the mast; we will get through this storm together." When you practice love every day and live in your heart, your judgments and fears will soften, and you will begin to trust that there is something bigger out there guiding you through this journey we call life. You will be able to tell the truth—to yourself and others—with ease and confidence. You will say yes to things that serve you, and no to things that drain you. And you will develop the courage to lift the veils of denial and truly see your life for what it is, and what it may become.

I know these concepts of self-love and self-worth may not always be easy in practice, especially if you have been traumatized. Think back to a time when someone or something triggered such a trauma in you. Your body may have felt like it was closing down. Your chest may have felt as if a cement block were resting on it, not allowing you to breathe. Or your stomach may have felt as if it were stapled shut, leaving you nauseated. Because experiencing these dark emotions was so visceral, it makes total sense why you cannot feel your light of self-love. But human experience is about accepting both the light and the dark, and facing your darkness is love in its most challenging form.

You may not think you can face your darkness, move through the sludge, and open yourself to love, but I promise you can. I promise you that when you try to connect to your heart, even a little, your intuition will give you the strength to look your trauma straight in the eyes and say, "I am not afraid of you anymore."

Let me help you. Here is a meditation you can use to connect to and open your fourth chakra, the heart chakra. Once you are able to open your heart chakra, you can direct this energy up into your sixth chakra, your third eye and the center of your intuition.

Close your eyes, take three deep breaths, and begin to relax. Now I want you to imagine a beautiful light moving through the body, clearing away anything negative that you are holding on to—fear, resentment, or anger. Have this light come straight to your heart and swirl around inside it. Treat your heart as if it were a flower, and you are opening each petal, giving the light greater access to your center. Notice how your body feels when it is open to the light and when you are in a place of the heart.

Now that you are in a place of the heart, in a place of love, think of a challenge you are facing. Feel all the emotions and heartache that surround this experience. Open your heart and bring in your hurt, trauma, and sadness. Let your heart embrace your challenge with love and acceptance. Let grief have a space in healing your pain. Now notice if you have a bit less pain, a bit more light, a bit more love for yourself and others. From this place of deep love, let this energy flow from your heart up into your third eye, the space right between your eyebrows. Your intuition resides in your sixth chakra and you will be able to home in on it by opening up this center. Notice how your body is feeling, how your heart is opening, and how your self-love and inner love are strengthening. Recognize how the energy in your mind, body, and spirit has shifted since your meditation began. Now slowly open your eyes and come back into the room.

I know this meditation will not take away all your pain and trauma, but it might remind you that you have a loving relationship with your intuition and an open channel to its wisdom. And it might give you a life jacket to hold on to when you feel you are drowning, and a "love flashlight" to shine into the dark corners of your life. This "love flashlight" can help you soften your depression, anxiety, grief, loss, and sadness.

By living in your intuition and accepting with compassion your fate, your story, and your pain, you also accept more of yourself. And when you accept more of yourself, you accept others as well. You don't look through eyes of bias at gender or race; you don't focus on age or agility, or bank accounts or bankruptcy. No, you look at people from a state of love that changes the world. It is your love that may end child sexual abuse, or your compassion that builds a well in a remote village. It is your concern for political corruption that may lead to a new law based upon honest principles.

Luke spoke of an all-encompassing kind of love in the Bible: "Love your enemies, do good to those who hate you, bless those who curse you, pray for those who mistreat you. If someone slaps you on one cheek, turn to them the other also. If someone takes your coat, do not withhold your shirt from them. Give to everyone who asks you, and if anyone takes what belongs to you, do not demand it back. Do to others as you would have them do to you."

Jesus also spoke of this type of love in Matthew 5:43–46: "You have heard that it was said, 'Love your neighbor and hate your enemy.' But I tell you, love your enemies and pray for those who persecute you." It is not easy to love all. Believe me, I struggle with this concept, but when I do choose to love all, I feel more connected to the human spirit, more connected to my intuitive heart.

The Greeks have a word for this type of love: "agape," a selfless love that extends to all people regardless of how you feel about them or what they have done in their life. Its meaning goes beyond the mere idea of love, however, and into the manifestation of love and your actions of love.

When you express agape, you create a oneness, a collective love for all humans. The domino effect of this oneness is learning to love more of yourself—total self-love and self-acceptance, in the purest form. The kind of self-love where you can let go of your fears and foibles, your family's dogmas and fantasies. The kind of self-acceptance where you can let go of who you think you should be.

We all have a hunger to be loved and to love others. We are hungry because we are longing for something real and pure. Love can be nothing but real, because it is your direct connection to your god. And your connection to your god is in everything and everywhere—in nature, suffering, politics, and poverty. When Mother Teresa was asked about how she could take care of all the people, she said, "I only take care of the one," meaning she takes care of God, because she saw God in all humans and all their suffering.

When you open your heart to all of life—sunsets and storms, healers and haters—you will see we are all one, so much more alike than different. We are all addicted to something, ignorant of something, clouded by something, and resistant to something. We are all learning how to trust, believe, be patient, and know that the more we encompass self-love, the more we encompass our souls.

Your pilgrimage can remind you of the power of your dreams, like when you read about a woman who listened so deeply to hers it saved her life. Your journey can remind you of the power of listening, like when you read the heartbreaking story of a mother who had to become a warrior in order to endure the sexual-abuse case of her daughter. And finally this path is about the power of asking yourself daily, "Who am I?"—as Cindy does—in order to learn how to succeed as an N of 1.

Love gives our intuitive spirits the power and permission to do all these things. Some may call this selfish; I call it freedom. "When love speaks, the voice of all the gods makes heaven drowsy with the harmony," Biron says in Shakespeare's *Love's Labour's Lost*. The gods will hear you and open up heaven for you to manifest all that you were put on this planet to do. Become alive with ecstasy, cry from the beauty of your soul, embrace mystery and the unknown, and direct a healing force into all your dark corners and crevasses. Feel Mother Earth's magnetic force and grace in your heart. Do all of this from love. Do this all from your intuition.

EPILOGUE

Writing this book I was reminded that as humans we all struggle. We all want to make good decisions. We all want to be loved and love others. I have learned that it is our intuition that moves us forward, even when we do not want to be mobile.

It is intuition that helps us begin picking up the rubble and shoveling dirt after a catastrophic earthquake.

It is intuition that gets us to an AA meeting after a night of drinking and breaking our sobriety.

It is intuition that forces us to listen to a dream because we knew something was not right in our body.

It is intuition that allows us to hear the name of someone we have met only once, but know is having an affair with our partner.

It is intuition that encourages us to book a ticket to India even though the voices around us are saying not to travel and leave our family.

It is intuition that gets us out of bed to feed our children the day after a partner commits suicide.

It is intuition that allows us to plan a loved one's funeral only minutes after they have died.

This is all intuition. Intuition is not one thing; it is many things, looks many ways, and has many layers. It is our intuition that gives us faith to know that we are students and teachers of life. We are continually on a path of discovery, and our life is more alive when we know our spiritual work is never done.

We are coming to the end of this book but another chapter of our life. The chapter where we put intuition at the forefront of our existence.

SELECTED BIBLIOGRAPHY

Agness, Karin. "Don't Buy Into The Gender Pay Gap Myth." Forbes Opinion, April 12, 2016, https://www.forbes.com/sites/karinagness/2016/04/12/dont-buy-into-the-gender-pay-gap-myth/#632062a22596.

Alleyne, Richard. "Welcome to the Information Age—174 Newspapers a Day." *Telegraph* (UK), February 11, 2011, http://www.telegraph.co.uk/news/science/science-news/8316534/Welcome-to-the-information-age-174-newspapers-a-day.html.

Assisi. Quoted in Louis Nizer, *Between You and Me*. [New York?]: Beechurst Press, 1948.

Barbour, Julian. *The End of Time: The Next Revolution in Physics*. New York: Oxford University Press, 1999.

Branson, Richard. Quoted in Guy Rigby, From Vision to Exit: The Entrepreneur's Guide to Building and Selling a Business. Great Britain: Harriman House Ltd., 2011.

Brower, Elena. *Personal communication. September 8, 2016.*

Buddha. Quoted in Patti Digh, *Life Is a Verb: 37 Days to Wake Up, Be Mindful, and Live Intentionally*. Guilford, CT: The Globe Pequot Press, 2008.

Chödrön, Pema. *Start Where You Are: A Guide to Compassionate Living*. Boston: Shambhala Publications, 1994.

Chopra, Deepak. *The Book of Secrets: Unlocking the Hidden Dimensions of Your Life*. New York: Three Rivers Press, 2004.

Coelho, Paulo. "Pauli Coelho: The Alchemy of Pilgramage." By Krista Tippett. *On Being*, podcast transcript, August 4, 2016, http://onbeing.org/programs/paulo-coelho-the-alchemy-of-pilgrimage/.

Dalai Lama. Quoted in Geraldine Appel, *Nothing Is Impossible: Build a New Life in Seven Stages*. Bloomington, IN: AuthorHouse UK, 2016.

———. Quoted in Trilok Chandra Majupuria and Indra Majupuria, *Tibet, a Guide to the Land of Fascination: An Overall Perspective of the Ancient, Medieval, and Modern* Periods. N.p.: S. Devi, 1988.

DeHaven, James M. *The 7 Gifts of Paradise: A Spiritual Guide to Understanding the Miracle of Life, the World, and Why We Are Here*. [Interlaken, NJ?]: JMD Productions, 2012.

Francis, John. *Planetwalker*. N.p.: Elephant Mountain Press, 2005.

Gandhi, Mahatma. Quoted in Andrew Holmes, *Ralph Waldo Emerson's Self-Reliance: A Modern-Day Interpretation of a Self-Help Classic*. Oxford, UK: Infinite Ideas Limited, 2010.

Goldsworthy, Andy. Quoted in Gregory Ripley, *Tao of Sustainability: Cultivate Yourself to Heal the Earth*. St. Petersburg, FL: Three Pines Press, 2016.

Hoomans, Joel. "35,000 Decisions: The Great Choices of Strategic Leaders." *Leading Edge Journal* on the website of Roberts Wesleyan College, March 20, 2015, http://go.roberts.edu/leadingedge/the-great-choices-of-strategic-leaders.

Jobs, Steve. Quoted b John C Abell, 'Steve Jobs,' Steve Jobs, And Me. October 27, 2011. Wired.com

Jung, Carl. *Memories, Dreams, Reflections*. Edited by Aniela Jaffe. Translated by Richard Winston and Clara Winston. New York: Random House, 1961.

———. *Psychology and Alchemy*. 12th volume. Edited and translated by Gerhard Adler and R. F. C. Hull. Princeton, NJ: Princeton University Press, 1968.

Kant, Immanuel. *Critique of Pure Reason*. Germany, 1781.

Koontz, Dean. *The Darkest Evening of the Year*. New York: Bantam Dell, 2007.

La Ligue de la Sainte-Messe. "Peace Prayer of Saint Francis." *La Clochette* (n.d., ca. 1912).

Lao Tzu. Quoted in Student Academy, *Words of Wisdom: Lao Tzu*. N.p.: Student Academy, 2015.

L'Engle, Madeline. *A Wrinkle in Time*. New York: Square Fish, 1962.

Lesser, Elizabeth. *Broken Open: How Difficult Times Can Help Us Grow*. New York: Villard Books, 2004.

Kornfield, Jack. *Buddha's Little Instruction Book*. New York: Bantam Books, 1994.

Machado, Antonio. *Border of a Dream: Selected Poems*. Translated by Willis Barnstone. Port Townsend, WA: Copper Canyon Press, 2004.

Medland, Dina. "Today's Gender Reality In Statistics, Or Making Leadership Attractive To Women." March 7, 2016. https://. www.forbes.com/sites/dinamedland/2016/03/07/todays-gen-der-reality-in-statistics-or-making-leadership-attractive-to-women/#17c307616883.

Milne, A. A. Quoted in Benjamin Hoff, *The Tao of Pooh*. New York: Penguin, 1982.

Muir, John. "Mountain Thoughts." In *John of the Mountains: The Unpublished Journals of John Muir* by Linnie Marsh Wolfe, ed. Madison, WI: University of Wisconsin Press, 1938.

O'Donahue, John. *Divine Beauty: The Invisible Embrace*. New York: HarperCollins, 2004.

Petroff, Alanna. "The Exact Age When Girls Lose Interest in Science and Math." *CNN Tech*, February 28, 2017, http://money.cnn.com/2017/02/28/technology/girls-math-science-engineering/.

Popova, Maria. "Einstein, Annie Lamott, and Steve Jobs on Intuition vs. Rationality." January 12, 2012, https://www.theatlantic.com/

entertainment/archive/2012/01/einstein-anne-lamott-and-steve-jobs-on-intuition-vs-rationality/251295.

Rumi. Quoted in Ed Conrad, *Heart Power: Inspiring the Courage to Heal and Love Yourself One Day at a Time*. Bloomington, IN: Balboa Press, 2014.

———. Quoted in Larry Chang, *Wisdom for the Soul: Five Millennia of Prescriptions for Spiritual Healing*. Washington, DC: Gnosophia Publishers, 2006.

———. Quoted in Nerisha Maharej, *Self-Love: The Authentic Path to Conscious Leadership*.

Salzberg, Sharon. "Sit." November 1, 2002. Oprah Magazine.

Shakespeare, William. *Love's Labour's Lost*. Act 4, sc. 3.

Singer, Michael A. *The Untethered Soul: The Journey Beyond Yourself*. Oakland, CA: New Harbinger Publications and Noetic Books, 2007.

The Women's Sports Foundation. "Title IX Myths and Facts." March 18, 2013 https://www.womenssportsfoundation.org/advocate/title-ix-issues/what-is-title-ix/title-ix-myths-facts/.

Turner, Kelly. "The Science Behind Intuition: Why You Should Trust Your Gut." *Psychology Today*, May 20, 2014, https://www.psychologytoday.com/blog/radical-remission/201405/the-science-behind-intuition.

University of Leeds. "Go with Your Gut—Intuition Is More Than Just a Hunch, Says New Research." *ScienceDaily*, March 6, 2008, www. sciencedaily.com/releases/2008/03/080305144210.htm.

Weisul, Kimber. "Globally, women gain corporate board seats— but not in the US." Fortune, January 12, 2015, http://fortune. com/2015/01/13/catalyst-women-boards-countries-us/.

Whitman, Walt. "I Sing the Body Electric." In *Leaves of Grass*. 1867.

Winfrey, Oprah. Quoted Kathryn Tristan, Anxiety Rescue: Simple Strategies to Stop Fear from Ruling Your Life. Chesterfield, MO: Dancing Eagle Press, 2010

Wordsworth, William. Quoted in Craig Brian Larson and Brian Lowery, *1001 Quotations That Connect: Timeless Wisdom for Preaching, Teaching, and Writing*. Grand Rapids, MI: Zondervan, 2009.

ACKNOWLEDGMENTS

Deep love and gratitude to my husband, Adam, whose selfless love and immense support are what keep me writing, laughing, and believing. I love you.

My son, Tommy, whose sensitive heart, loving spirit, and dedication to life teach me every day how to love on a deeper level with compassion.

My daughter, Cora, who teaches me about courage and following one's intuitive soul. You show me a path of living with bravery and creativity.

My mom. I would not be me without you. You have taught me how to give, love, be a mother, and follow my heart. I love and thank you.

My dad. Even though you have passed away, you will forever live in my heart and soul.

My sister and best friend, Kelly. You hold me up when I cannot stand, make me laugh when I want to cry, and have supported my ever-changing journey.

My beloved family: my brothers, Tommy, Michael, and Leo; my sisters-in-law, Meghan, Christie, Betsy, Jess, and Sharon; my two nieces and eleven nephews; my mothers-in-law, Sue and Jeannine; and my fathers-in-law, Dana and Bob. I love you all so dearly.

My agent and friend, Victoria Wells. Thank you for following your gut one fall day in New York City.

My publishers, Amazon and Grand Harbor Press, in particular Erin Calligan Mooney. Your support, wisdom, and belief in me will never be forgotten.

My editor, Sarah Faulkner, whose brilliant mind and heartfelt wisdom gave more life to *Trust Within*. And to my copyeditor, Matthew Patin, and my proofreader, Katie Allison, thank you.

My devoted reader, Tory, this book would not have happened without your love and commitment.

My fellow warrior writers, Nicole and Kim, thank you for all your unending love and support.

My women friends who are an integral part of my heart: Charlotte H., Hilary, Jen, Meghan P., Jordana, Jill, Molly, Megan S., Cady, René, Johanna, Charlotte G., Jenny, Noelle, Julia, Krissy, Bridget, Cynthia, Tiffiney, Michelle, Amy, Lisa, Amanda, Kirstin, my Omaha tribe from Saint Joan of Arc, and my fellow crusaders from Marian High School.

My friend and mentor Rob McDonald at Apple, who in the beginning of my writing career believed in me and gave me the confidence I needed to trust I could be a writer. I am forever grateful.

The brave souls who let me tell their stories: John, Jay, Suzanne, Jenny, Austyn, Linda, Trisha, Cindy, Sunny, Neal, and Peter. There would be no book without your trust within.

To the things that keep me going: my spiritual guides, prayer, meditation, God, yoga, my therapist Nancy, and the world of nature. All of which inspire my soul so that words can flow through my body and onto the page.

ABOUT THE AUTHOR

Molly Carroll is a nonfiction writer, artist, educator, and therapist who holds a master's degree in counseling psychology. She is an expert in her field, with more than twenty years of experience in education and mental health. Molly wrote and developed the artistic self-help journal *Cracking Open*, which draws on her own professional and personal experience as a therapist, mother, and daughter, as well as her life in the small community of Bend, Oregon.

Molly's 2015 TEDx talk was widely viewed. She conducts popular workshops with women and families throughout the West Coast and Costa Rica. Molly is a successful public speaker for corporations, teachers, administrators, and physicians. For more on the author and her work, visit www.molly-carroll.com.